—————— MIND MATTERS ——————

Mad or Bad?

——— MIND MATTERS ———

Series editor: Judith Hughes

In the same series

—————— MIND MATTERS ——————

mad or bad?

MICHAEL BAVIDGE

PUBLISHED BY BRISTOL CLASSICAL PRESS

Printed in Great Britain

First published in 1989 by:

Bristol Classical Press,
226 North Street,
Bedminster,
Bristol BS3 1JD.

Text © Michael Bavidge, 1989
Cartoons © Adrian Barclay, 1989

British Library Cataloguing in Publication Data

Bavidge, Michael
Mad or Bad? (Mind Matters)
1. Man. Actions. Responsibility
I. Title II. Series
170

ISBN 1-85399-016-7
ISBN 1-85399-017-5 Pbk

for the students of philosophy
at the Centre for Continuing Education
Newcastle University

contents

foreword

'A philosophical problem has the form *I don't know my way about*,' said Wittgenstein. These problems are not the ones where we need information, but those where we are lost for lack of adequate signposts and landmarks. Finding our way – making sense out of the current confusions and becoming able to map things both for ourselves and for others – is doing successful philosophy. This is not quite what the lady meant who told me when I was seven that I ought to have more philosophy, because philosophy was eating up your cabbage and not making a fuss about it. But that lady *was* right to suggest that there were some useful skills here.

Philosophizing, then, is not just a form of highbrow chess for postgraduate students; it is becoming conscious of the shape of our lives, and anybody may need to do it. Our culture contains an ancient tradition which is rich in helpful ways of doing so, and in Europe they study that tradition at school. Here, that study is at present being squeezed out even from university courses. But that cannot stop us doing it if we want to. This series contains excellent guide-books for people who do want to, guide-books which are clear, but which are not superficial surveys. They are themselves pieces of real philosophy, directed at specific problems which are likely to concern all of us. Read them.

MARY MIDGLEY

preface

Philosophers are very good at talking to one another. Some of them are also good at talking with other people. In the market-places of Athens, the cafés of Paris, and lately, in the pubs of London, philosophers have always found a public bursting with its own ideas and keen to discuss them with others. The need to ask and attempt to answer philosophical questions is in us all and is prompted sometimes by particular events in our personal lives and sometimes by a more general unease about wider social or political or scientific issues. At such times there is always a popular demand for philosophers to explain themselves and the views of their illustrious forebears in ways which others can understand and question and use.

It is not an easy thing to do because Philosophy is not easy, though its central insights, like those in the sciences, are often startingly simple. To gain those insights we all have to follow the paths of reasoning for ourselves. Signposts have been left for us by the great philosophers of the past, and deciphering some of them is part of the business of this series.

'Mind Matters' is not 'Philosophy Made Easy' but rather 'Philosophy Made Intelligible', and the authors in this series have been chosen for more than their philosophical knowledge. Some of them are also experts in other fields such as medicine, computing or biology. All are people who recognise and try to practise the art of writing in an accessible and clear manner, believing that philosophical thought which is not under-standable is best kept to oneself. Many have acquired this ability in the harsh discipline of adult education where students bring their own knowledge and puzzles to the subject and demand real explanations of relevant issues.

Each book in this series begins with a perplexing question that we may ask ourselves without, perhaps, realising that we are 'philosophising': Do computers have minds? Can a pile of bricks be a work of art? Should we hold pathological killers responsible for their crimes? Such questions are considered and new questions raised with frequent reference to the views of major philosophers. The authors go further than this, however. It is not their intention to produce a potted history of philosophical ideas. They also make their own contributions to the subject, suggesting different avenues of thought to explore. The result is a collection of original writings on a wide range of topics produced for all those who find Philosophy as fascinating and compelling as they do.

Michael Bavidge's question, 'Mad or Bad?', arises out of a long-standing philosophical interest in the connections between ethics and the philosophy of mind and from surprise at the verdicts in some notorious murder trials.

Dreadful crimes demand total, unreserved condemnation and heavy punishment, but their dreadfulness also leads us to think, 'Anyone who does *that* must be nuts!'

This book provides a thought-provoking and sensitive new attempt to show us how we can preserve our ordinary moral intuitions about dreadful crimes while facing up to the difficulties of holding psychopathic criminals fully responsible for their actions. It is an important topic with wide-ranging implications which affect us all.

JUDITH HUGHES

acknowledgements

I am indebted to all those who have taught philosophy at Newcastle University in recent years, particularly to Geoff and Mary Midgley for their kindness and encouragement, and to Alan Greenwood-Wilson for his philosophical comradeship. I have been greatly helped by discussions with Judy Hughes, Jane Heal and Ian Ground. The original article out of which this book developed appeared in the inaugural edition of the *Journal of Applied Philosophy* and I am grateful to Brenda Almond and Richard Tur for the help they gave me. Finally, I wish to thank Edgar Wilson for the constant stimulation that he has given me by refusing to believe a word of it.

1: the problem

reactions to gross depravity

On May 22nd 1981, Peter Sutcliffe, known as the Yorkshire Ripper, was found guilty on thirteen charges of murder. The next day, *The Times* reported that 'when the news of the verdicts reached the crowds in Old Bailey, outside the court, there were three cheers for the jury'. As acquittal was not a possibility, the cheering can only have been for the jury's rejection of the alternative verdict of manslaughter due to diminished responsibility.

Inside the court the journalist, David Yallop, heard the same verdicts. His account of that moment sounds as if he interpreted the jury's decision as a personal vindication:

> At eight minutes past four the jury have returned. They have reached a majority verdict. Peter William Sutcliffe is found guilty of murder on all thirteen counts. No madness. No voices from God. No divine mission. He has been declared sane. He is evil.
> (Yallop, 1981, p. 361)

The day following the verdict, *The Guardian* published an article on the trial. The writer, Edward Fitzgerald, made no attempt to hide his resentment at the affront to his sensibilities that the verdict represented, nor his contempt for those whose sensibilities are different:

> The only point of the trial, then, was to determine the issue of responsibility: or rather to justify that edifying climax of condemnation in which the imprecation of the words 'guilty' and 'murder' are meant to serve as some solace to the vengeful for the absence of the black cap and the death sentence.

1

These are examples of the way our society splits over the issue of whether psychopathic killers are, to use the irresistible phrase, mad or bad. The split occurs not only between those who think of themselves as conservatives and those who see themselves as progressives. It can emerge within one mind. On December 21st 1977, Bernard Levin published an article in *The Times* in which he commented on 'the confusion that surrounds – indeed, that constitutes – our society's attitude to imprisonment and the reasons for it'. In the course of his remarks, he offers the following thoughts on the notorious child-killers known as the Moors Murderers:

> The deterrent effect of the life sentence imposed on Miss Hindley and Mr Brady for the appalling crimes of which they were both justly convicted, is and always was, obviously *nil*. The origins of the impulses that drove them to such evil are buried deep in the human psyche; whatever they may be, they are not to be reached by any probe of reason. Those capable not only of conceiving but of carrying out sadistic practices of the kind involved in their case are incapable of weighing the consequences for their victims, or indeed of understanding them...Lord Longford, who has visited Miss Hindley frequently, and a recently released prisoner who had seen much of her in prison, are both convinced that she genuinely repented of her crimes, and would be no danger to society or anyone in it if she were now released.

(Levin, 1980, p. 222)

This passage is characteristic of things we are driven to say when we try to be realistic and humane in the face of gross depravity. It contains a number of paradoxes. The most obvious tension concerns Myra Hindley's responsibility. Mr. Levin seems to think she was responsible – how else could she be 'justly convicted' and later 'genuinely repent of her crimes'? But he also believes she was not responsible – how could she be, driven as she was by deep impulses, 'incapable of weighing the consequences for their victims, or indeed of understanding them'?

Conflicting reactions like these occur whenever a sensational crime of a psychopathic nature comes to light. Inevitably such crimes evoke outrage, fear and hatred. The outrage is at its strongest in the rare cases where a psychopathic killer is known to be at large. The crimes are often of a particularly brutal nature. Frequently the targets of the psychopath are known, women, or children, or the elderly, or members of a particular racial group. Such knowledge, combined with the impossibility of defending oneself or one's dependents against unprovoked attack from an unknown source, maximises the fear and resentment. Sometimes the outrage spills over into conflict within the law-abiding community, as occurred between feminist groups and the police in some Yorkshire towns, during the period when Peter Sutcliffe was conducting his murderous attacks.

The killings we are considering have been called serial murders to distinguish them from other forms of multiple killing. They are not the same as the mass killings perpetrated on one occasion by a rampaging assailant. They are repetitive killings carried out by someone who resorts to homicide as a strategy for handling psychological problems. It has been estimated (Holmes and De Burger, 1988, pp. 12-21) that in America between 3,500 and 5,000 people are killed annually by serial murderers. They guess that there are about 350 such killers at large in America at any given time. Given a total figure of 18,692 murders in 1984, it is clear that serial killing is a significant and growing problem at least in United States. These figures are of course informed guesses. Reliable statistics are difficult to obtain because it is not always clear which deaths or disappearances are to be put down to the multiple murderer. Usually, the crimes only come to light on the arrest of the culprit.

The fact that to a considerable extent serial killing is hidden explains why it does not cause even more alarm than it does at present. However, even when people have not had to live under the shadow of unpredictable attack, the hatred kindled by these offences can be extreme. Decades after the crimes, the animosity towards the criminal can still reach dangerous levels.

These immediate reactions of revulsion and anger are reflected in the rhetoric of the press. On the whole, the more popular and populist the paper, the more it expresses the traditional reaction of hatred and vindictiveness. It is interesting to observe how in their search for the superlatives of condemnation, headline writers describe the criminal in non-human terms. They draw on the sub- and the super-human for revealing analogies. The criminal is a beast or a demon. He has dropped out of human society into the animal world, or he has been possessed by an alien force of superhuman malignity. Clearly such rhetoric must be restrained if traditional retributive and punitive attitudes are to be maintained. We want human beings, not animals or fallen angels in the dock.

Strong feelings are not restricted to the popular press nor to the crowds that gather outside law courts to hurl abuse and missiles at notorious criminals. Professionals, whose views, practices and interests are at stake when such cases come to court, arise to protect their investment. We have already seen the two broad camps into which their responses fall. They can be fairly called the traditional and the progressive. The traditionalists are suspicious of the progressive's tendency to medicalise wickedness. A fastidious concern with the criminal's mental state manifests, in their eyes, the moral ambiguity of modern society in an unholy alliance with the self-interest of elitist professionals, such as psychiatrists and social workers. The traditionalists tend to equate concern with the decency of our treatment of criminals with lack of sympathy for their victims. They are also inclined to interpret a willingness to raise questions about responsibility with an unwillingness to protect society from the violent and depraved. For this reason there is never a shortage of the more robust traditionalists volunteering to operate the gallows, should the public executioner be overcome by qualms of conscience.

The progressives, on the other hand, are quick to accuse the law of incoherence. They expect the law to be incoherent because they see it as an expression of outmoded attitudes of vindictiveness and retribution. They tend to interpret all enigmas and confusions concerning responsibility as evidence on their side. If we experience difficulties in reaching decisions about culpability it is because the moral and legal concepts involved embody the beliefs of a pre-scientific world view. Any inadequacies in their own accounts are written off as the inevitable result of the youth of psychiatry, or as the consequence of the way in which psychiatry is inevitably compromised when it appears in the witness box. They react strongly because they see the incurably retributive procedures of the law not only as an assault on the mentally sick, but as an affront to the reputation and authority of psychiatry which are, they believe, integral to a modern, decent society.

It may be suggested that the attitudes of both parties are defensible and that all they disagree over is the application of their various judgements to this or that particular criminal, or class of criminal. We cannot expect that there should be no borderline cases. Both the progressives and the traditionalists allow an insanity defence. They disagree only about whether this individual or that class of individuals (for example, those normally labelled 'psychopathic') falls into a relevant category.

Unfortunately, the disagreement between the two parties does not take the form of an argument about borderlines. In disputes over borderline cases, there is common understanding of the general concepts that are being used and broad agreement about the criteria for their application. The disagreement is simply, for example, whether this man has just too much hair to count as bald. There is no falling out over the meaning of baldness or the technique of counting hairs. The dispute between the Mad and the Bad parties, however, exhibits differences of principle and approach. Susanne Dell reports a case in which two psychiatrists disagreed about an offender's responsibility for his crimes although they agreed in diagnosing him as a hysterical psychopath. She offers a general comment on her survey of cases in 1976 and 1977:

> ...although the presence or absence of mental responsibility is not a medical matter, doctors grapple with it: and in half the cases where they disagreed with each other on the issue of diminished responsibility, it was on the moral and not the psychiatric aspects of the case that they disagreed.
>
> (Dell, 1982, p. 813)

While there may be room for borderline disagreements in the

The disagreement is simply whether this man has just too much hair to count as bald.

psychological assessment, there seems no possibility of compromise in the moral responses. According to some, the psychopathic offender is the paradigm of wickedness; according to others he is clearly not fully responsible for what he has done. So this attempt to placate both sides misrepresents the nature of the dispute and will satisfy neither protagonist.

There is a third party to the debate: those who cry 'a plague on both your houses'. Whether the psychopathic killer is responsible for his acts or not is an arcane point which philosophers and others who enjoy that sort of thing can discuss indefinitely. The practical problem is to restrain such antisocial characters. This can be done independently of whatever views are held about their responsibility. This no-nonsense approach seems specially convincing when the fate of the criminal is unaffected by the decision concerning responsibility. Prior to the abolition of the death penalty in Britain, the very life of the criminal hung in the balance as the jury decided between murder and manslaughter. After abolition, in the cases of psychopathic killings, the outcome for the accused may very well be the same in either case. So, asks the pragmatist, what is all the fuss about?

The original purpose in introducing the new *verdict* of manslaughter due to diminished responsibility, was to effect a change in *sentence,* namely to free certain classes of killers from the death penalty. Now, after the abolition of the death penalty, the suggestion is that the reason for the special verdict no longer exists.

From a practical point of view this is a dangerous argument. The death penalty has been reintroduced in many American states. As I write this paragaph, the British House of Commons is discussing the *eighteenth* attempt in twenty-three years to reintroduce execution into the British penal system. Homicide law is difficult to change, and that includes the verdicts that are available to a jury. Penalties, on the other hand, can be altered with ease. It would be unwise to dismantle the various defences that would stand between a convicted killer and execution, were the death penalty reintroduced.

There is a more general criticism of the diminished responsibility plea, which bears on the relationship between verdict and sentence, but which does not depend on whether the death penalty is in force or not. The considerations concerning responsibility, which currently are presented to the jury as they decide their verdict, could, it is suggested, be dealt with after the verdict by the sentencing authorities when they come to decide the disposal of the convicted person. Under this arrangement the jury need only consider whether or not the accused did the deeds which form the basis of the charge.

There are, no doubt, advantages in such an arrangement. The most respectable reason for taking these decisions in committee is to escape from the adversarial structure of the criminal trial. The least respectable is that these issues, which look suspiciously undecidable and yet have to be decided, had better be decided in private. What is not in dispute is that the point of such an arrangement is to ensure that the issues of responsibility are not entrusted to a jury but are decided by doctors, psychiatrists, social workers and lawyers.

It is a deeply embedded assumption of the law that responsibility is not a scientific matter, nor is its ascription a matter of expertise. If this assumption is sound, there is no reason to believe that medical experts are better placed than anyone else to determine the matter. There are no experts in responsibility. Whether or not an individual is responsible for his criminal actions is a substantial issue concerning personality and relationships that ought to go to the jury.

the law and morality
The pragmatist opposes the current homicide law because he is suspicious of the way in which it appeals to an unmistakably moral notion of responsibility. His opposition to this particular piece of legislation is only part of a general policy which is to minimize the relationship between the law and morality.

The precise way in which moral issues impinge on the homicide law we must explain later. But now, at the beginning of our enquiry, we should remind ourselves to what extent English common law and other legal systems, which are related to it, are permeated by moral considerations. It is, of course, true that crime is not the same thing as sin, nor legal liability the same as moral responsibility, nor *mens rea* (the *guilty mind* required by most offences) the same as a guilty conscience. Many acts are immoral but not illegal; many acts are illegal but not immoral. Morality has always been concerned with personal motives and intentions. In recent morality there has been a shift towards an ultra-pure sense of responsibility, according to which someone is to be blamed only for those aspects of their behaviour which are attributable entirely to their own initiatives. The law, on the other hand, is an instrument of social control. Preoccupation with the issues of responsibility concern 'the fine feelings of the soul'. Whereas the practical problem that the criminal, particularly the multiple killer, presents to society must be resolved according to 'the harsh and rugged dictates of political utility' (Bentham, J., 1970, p. 25).

In these and other ways, morality and the law diverge. Yet it remains true that English common law, and other related legal systems, are shot through with moral considerations. A crime has always been thought of as a wicked act. The heart of the criminal law concerns the 'ethical minimum', murder, rape, theft, fraud, acts which are universally, or well-nigh universally condemned. If the law is to be deployed against anyone, it ought to attend to those whose behaviour is antisocial in these fundamental ways. There is a corresponding reluctance to put well-meaning citizens outside the law by injudicious legislation, which criminalizes innocent behaviour. Equally, on the other hand, there are moves to decriminalize behaviour which no longer attracts moral condemnation.

Just as there is pressure to align crimes and wicked acts, so there is pressure to align moral responsibility with criminal liability. In 1953 the Royal Commission on Capital Punishment expressed this requirement in a strong statement:

> Responsibility is a moral question; and there is no issue on which it is more important that the criminal law should be in close accord with the moral standards of the community. There can be no pre-established harmony between the criteria of moral and of criminal responsibility, but they ought to be made to approximate as nearly as possible.
>
> (Cmnd 8932, §281)

All legal systems make some accommodation for the mentally ill. These measures are taken to protect those who are not responsible for their actions from the rigours of the law. For similar reasons, we feel uncomfortable about statutory offences which require no element of *mens rea*, and therefore no element of personal responsibility. If they are tolerated, it is because in some cases public utility is thought to be worth injustice to individuals.

Punishment is the ultimate reason why the law and morality can never be kept apart. It is not just that punishment has been traditionally justified in retributive terms, nor that the severity of punishment has been determined by considering the extent of the public harm caused by the crime and the personal malice of the criminal. All of these factors are unavoidably moral. However punishment forges a closer connection between morality and the law than even these considerations suggest. The criminal law is always about punishment. It may even be that between crime and punishment there is a logical connection. If it is only possible to define a crime as that which is subject to criminal procedures, and if, in turn, it is only possible to define criminal procedures as those that issue in punishment, then the idea of punishment is built into the very foundations of criminal law. However, even if these logical connections are challenged, no-one would wish to deny that, in practice, punishment is what the criminal law comes down to in the end.

Punishments are evils or harms deliberately inflicted on people. They are real, objective harms – fines, imprisonment, humiliations, mutilations, death – they are not penalties which only count as penalties because of the rules of the game. They are not like sliding down a snake in Ludo, or paying a fine in Monopoly money. For this reason, legal positivism, which defends the view that law and morality are radically separate enterprises, cannot be correct. Because punishments are real harms, the imposition of criminal penalties demands moral justification. Consequently, the processes that lead to the imposition of those penalties, which include the decision procedures which determine who is to be punished, for what actions, and with what severity, must be morally defensible.

It is not sufficient that the law be morally defensible, as it were from the outside. The playing of Ludo may be justified as an innocent pastime, without claiming that the game is permeated by moral considerations. The law, on the other hand, must not only be justifiable as an institution, but must incorporate moral standards, ideals and principles, which regulate the imposition of punishments, because the penalties that it imposes are real harms.

So the positivist who, in his efforts to avoid what he sees as undecidable issues in morals or metaphysics, asks us to separate moral from legal questions does not reflect the actual state of the criminal law. We shall see that his position is incompatible in particular with the homicide law, which makes special demands concerning assessments of responsibility. He can continue to claim that it would be better if the law were purged of all moral elements. It may be more sensible, however, both from the practical point of view and from the point of view of principle, to face up to the difficulties that attach to our notion of responsibility, rather than to advise that the law try to manage without the idea.

the law and philosophy

Even when it is acknowledged that the law is not divorced, in principle, from moral considerations, there may still be a reluctance to look to the law for any enlightenment on issues of morality and responsibility. The law, it may be thought, is ideologically committed to an antiquated retributive morality or to an equally antiquated folk psychology of freedom and responsibility. Or, the claim may be, the law is a blunt instrument of social control. Morality is concerned with the individual, with personal motivation, responsibility and guilt, whereas the law enforces a minimum standard of acceptable behaviour on the community as a whole. It has neither the resources nor the need to attend to the individual aspects of human action. Such views may be reinforced by a political judgement that the law is the expression of the will of the dominant section of society, and has no greater claim to be regarded as a source of moral insight than any other manifestation of power.

David Hume expressed his scepticism about the value of combining legal and philosophical considerations in a letter to Adam Smith. He was commenting on a book written by his friend Lord Kames:

> I am afraid of Kames' *Law Tracts*. A man might as well think of making a fine sauce by a mixture of wormwood and aloes, as an agreeable composition by joining metaphysics and Scottish law.

> (Quoted in Mossner, 1954, p. 411)

The philosopher who discusses issues of responsibility and the law takes on the thankless task of stalking the borderlands between law, psychiatry and philosophy, which like most border territories are matters of wars and disputes, of danger and confusion. They are also the areas where changes occur.

No-one should give the law overriding authority in moral matters. It is perfectly proper to be sceptical about the claim that the law exhibits a deeper understanding of moral concepts than is available to untutored commonsense. Still, the judgements made in law have considerable advantages over either the everyday judgements we make of each other's conduct or the opinions expressed by philosophical theorists.

Unlike the philosopher, the courts are required to come to decisions in particular cases within a restricted time. This may lead to some rough justice. But it ensures that legal decisions retain their connection with the practicalities of life. The conceptual resources of the law have at least survived in a decision-making environment. The courts, unlike, for example, parents in relation to children, have to apply the same general rules across a very broad spectrum of cases. They have to face repeated public tests of fairness and impartiality. In particular, the law has to give explicit reasons for its judgements. Though the law is an exercise of power, and though standardly it is an embodiment of the conventional values of society, it can be neither silently. It is committed to giving public reasons for its decisions. What in everyday morality goes unsaid, struggles for expression in the law. The result is that those who reflect on moral concepts and beliefs can find in the law a publicly available source of judgements, and a repository of the ideas, distinctions and beliefs that underlie them.

The purpose of this book is to face up to the problems that serial killers present. This enterprise will engage us in legal and philosophical enquiries. It demands that we come to a decision about our attitude to serial killers and that we make explicit the philosophical basis of our decision. In particular, it requires that we achieve as clear an understanding as possible of the concepts of responsibility.

The law provides a starting point. Different legal systems have different homicide laws. Statutes in different states are framed differently. While referring to other systems, we will concentrate on English homicide law, which is based on the 1957 Homicide Act. Though it is, of course, only one example of homicide law, it is an important example which has influenced the law of many countries other than Britain. Furthermore, the differences between legal traditions can be exaggerated. They all have to face up to the same enigmas of extreme human behaviour that mass killers exhibit. They have, by and large, adopted the same set of strategies. We should start our study here, without assuming that these strategies embody eternal and irreformable insights into human nature and the moral life.

notes

Legal positivism is a view about the nature of law according to which what counts as law does not depend on the content of the law. In particular, there is no requirement, according to this theory, that the law embody any moral elements. Provided a rule has the recognised provenance, it qualifies as law irrespective of its merits.

Mens rea, literally 'guilty mind', refers to the blameworthy mental acts or states which are required if someone is to be found a guilty of a crime. The term covers the different intentions which are required for various offences. For example, the difference between murder and manslaughter often, though not always, turns on the intention with which the killing was carried out. *Mens rea* also refers to psychological aspects of behaviour which are not intentions, such as recklessness. The mass of law that has accumulated on the issue of *mens rea* is designed to bring to bear on particular types of offence the general principle that it is not sufficient for the commission of a crime that a person caused a harm: it is necessary that he did so with a blameworthy state of mind. We are reluctant to condemn someone whom we believe to be innocent from the personal, subjective point of view of their own intentions and motives. This is however not to say that a guilty verdict is only appropriate in cases where the culprit *feels* guilty.

Retributive punishment is punishment seen as a moral response to the guilt of the offender. Retribution is thought to be justified completely and only in terms of the desert of the criminal. Unlike utilitarian theories of punishment, it looks for justification neither to the deterrent nor reformative effects of punishment. Utilitarianism demands that all actions, including the imposition of punishments, be assessed in terms of their consequences; we should always act so as to maximize good consequences. A retributivist believes that we should only punish those who deserve punishment, and that those who deserve punishment, deserve it quite independently of any reference to the advantages or disadvantages that may follow on its imposition.

Retribution is distinguished by its advocates from vengeance, on the grounds that it is a requirement of justice, whereas vengeance gets what justification it can, from the fact that it provides psychological satisfaction to those who imagine themselves to be injured parties.

Books and articles referred to in this chapter:

Bentham, Jeremy, 1970, *An Introduction to the Principles of Morals and Legislation*, (London, The Athlone Press).

Dell, Susanne, 1982, 'Diminished Responsibility Reconsidered' *Criminal Law Review*, pp. 809-18.

Holmes, Ronald, M. and De Burger, James, 1988, *Serial Murder* (Newbury Park, Sage Publications).

Levin, Bernard, 1980, *Taking Sides* (London, Pan).

Mossner, Ernest, Campbell, 1954, *The Life of David Hume* (Edinburgh, Thomas Nelson and Son).

Royal Commission on Capital Punishment, 1953, Cmnd 8932.

Yallop, David, 1981, *Deliver Us From Evil* (London, Macdonald Futura Publishers).

2: diminished responsibility: the law

legal insanity and psychopathy

Psychopaths present us with a number of practical and theoretical problems, because it is not clear in what way their undoubted psychological abnormality ought to affect our moral and legal judgements about them.

In the case of people who satisfy the legal definition of insanity, their mental condition is such that few would deny that it constitutes a defence. The reason why insanity, in the legal sense, exonerates is that it involves serious, cognitive incapacities. (The term 'cognitive' refers exclusively to understanding and rationality.) The legally insane have an insecure grasp on the world, they do not understand the nature of their own acts, and they have a flawed appreciation of the social and penal world in which they live. The insane cannot attain objective information about or insight into their environment. Their perception of their own actions and situation is seriously distorted. It is true, as one judge put it, that:

> ...the mere fact that a man thinks he is John the Baptist does not entitle him to shoot his mother.
>
> (Smith and Hogan, 1973, p. 138)

However, if a man does believe he is John the Baptist, and if he shoots his mother, he is entitled to have his plea of insanity accepted as a complete defence.

We do not want to say that the insane person should be exonerated only in respect of those criminal acts which would not be criminal, were they in fact the acts that in his deluded state he took them to be. That is, the man who believes he is John the Baptist is excused whether or not his acts (as he perceives them) would be permissible acts (as we perceive them) for John the Baptist. The man who thinks he is John the Baptist is entitled not to be judged as if he were John the Baptist. Apart from any other consideration, the only act permissible now for John the Baptist is to keep very, very still.

The person whose belief system is so awry that our best attempt to express it is to say, 'he believes he is John the Baptist', is deluded to such an extent that no ascription of responsibility could be secure.

Such a position is difficult to maintain in the cases of psychopathic killers, who know what they are doing and intend to do it, whose acts are voluntary, and who appreciate that their crimes are universally condemned morally and legally.

I use the term 'psychopathic' because it is in general use to cover the sorts of cases I have in mind. The term has advantages and disadvantages. An advantage is that it makes explicit the psychogenic sources of the aberrant behaviour. In attempting to understand the behaviour of the psychopath it is to his beliefs, emotions and values that we must look. A term like 'sociopath' loses this connection, and consequently invites the criticism that the term is no more than a pseudo-medical expression for a bad person. The psychopathic personality is typically described as asocial, dominated by uncontrolled desires, impulsive, extremely aggressive if frustrated, incapable of normal affection and apparently feeling little if any guilt.

Ronald M. Holmes and James De Burger (Holmes and Burger, 1988, pp. 55-60), divide serial killers into four types:

the *visionary*, whose crimes are a response to voices or visions, and who for this reason could well count as psychotic, and therefore as criminally insane;

the *mission-orientated* who directs his attacks against a particular group of people perceived as undesirable;

the *hedonistic* whose primary motive is pleasure; among this group are the sexually motivated killers;

the *power/control orientated* in whom the principal driving force is the desire to dominate and for whom destruction is the ultimate expression of power.

It is not at all clear whether a killer who falls into any of these categories exhibits psychological characteristics that could provide him with a defence against a charge of murder. The cognitive incapacity that characterizes the legally insane is absent, except perhaps in the case of the visionary type. Yet all legal systems must face up to the problem of dealing with criminals whose unusual personalities at least raise the question of the appropriateness of a conviction for murder. The 1957 Homicide Act introduced into English law a defence based upon the mental abnormality of the accused which did not demand that the accused be legally insane. The question we are considering is whether psychopathic killers should be able to find protection under this Act.

the structure of section 2 of the act
The Homicide Act 1957, s. 2, says:

> (1) Where a person kills or is a party to the killing of another, he shall not be convicted of murder if he was suffering from such abnormality of mind (whether arising from a condition of arrested or retarded development of mind or any inherent causes or induced by disease or injury) as substantially impaired his mental responsibility for his acts and omissions in doing or being a party to the killing.
> (2) On a charge of murder, it shall be for the defence to prove that the person charged is by virtue of this section not liable to be convicted of murder.
> (3) A person who but for this section would be liable, whether as principal or as accessory, to be convicted of murder shall be liable instead to be convicted of manslaughter.

Critics of the Act accuse it of being obscure and of dealing in unintelligible concepts. But the logical structure underlying this piece of legislation is clear and simple. In the cases envisaged, the ultimate decision that the jury must make is whether the accused is to be convicted of murder or manslaughter. This decision is to depend on whether the 'mental responsibility' of the accused is substantially impaired or not. This issue, in turn, is to be decided by the degree of abnormality of mind that characterises the accused. So criminal liability depends on mental responsibility and mental responsibility depends on abnormality of mind.

The basic structure of the Act includes one psychological *assessment* and two *decisions* about responsibility, viz. one *attribution* of mental responsibility and one *verdict* which determines criminal liability.

It follows directly from the logic of section 2 that *criminal liability* is not the same thing as *mental responsibility*. The law assumes that there is a sort of responsibility which is different from the liability determined by the courts. It may be tempting in practice to ignore this point and interpret 'mental responsibility' as meaning 'liability to be convicted of murder rather than manslaughter'. Such an interpretation has the advantage of sidestepping difficult issues, but it has the disadvantage of making a nonsense of the section which says that 'mental responsibility' provides the basis on which criminal liability is to be attributed. It cannot therefore be true that the law is indifferent to types of personal responsibility other than that which is at stake when we decide whether someone is liable under the law.

The Homicide Act, for better or worse, is incompatible with the legal positivist view of the law. Legal positivists are committed to the view that the only sense of responsibility that concerns the courts must be definable in purely legal terms. The positivist may be right in thinking that the law ought to be so constructed, that we would be better off if it were so constructed. But he is wrong if he thinks that it is so constructed.

The Act does not tell us what *mental responsibility* is, though it implies that whatever it is, it varies. One can have more or less of it. It can be impaired and so, presumably, can flourish unimpaired. The degree of mental responsibility that one enjoys, may vary, so the Act assumes, depending on the abnormality of one's mind.

abnormality of mind

'Abnormality of mind' is another key phrase in the Act and it also is undefined. The phrase is to be understood in contrast to insanity, which gets its classic legal definition in the M'Naghten Rules:

> ...to establish a defence on the grounds of insanity, it must be clearly proved that, at the time of the committing of the act, the party accused was labouring under such a defect of reason, from disease of the mind, as not to know the nature and quality of the act he was doing; or, if he did know it, that he did not know he was doing what was wrong.

The traditional rationale behind the M'Naghten Rules has been stated by Lord Devlin in the following terms:

> As it is a matter of theory, I think there is something logical – it may be astringently logical, but it is logical – in selecting as the test of responsibility to the law, reason and reason alone. It is reason which makes a man responsible to the law. It is reason which gives him sovereignty over animate and inanimate things. It is what distinguishes him from the animals, which emotional disorder does not; it is what makes him man; it is what makes him subject to the law. So it is fitting that nothing other than a defect of reason should give complete absolution.
>
> (Smith and Hogan, 1973, p. 140)

Lord Devlin sets out to show that the test of legal responsibility should be in terms of 'reason and reason alone'. But his arguments do not establish that. They do not determine whether the ability to reason is a necessary or a sufficient ground for legal responsibility. Few would deny that only rational beings are subject to the law: no reasoning power, no liability. But the controversy over the M'Naghten Rules is about whether the ability to reason, so narrowly defined, is a *sufficient* basis on which to attribute responsibility. Even if we are convinced that legal responsibility is incurred precisely in virtue of the ability to reason about behaviour, the question remains: can the ability to apply reason to one's behaviour be captured in exclusively rational terms? Must we not consider also the individual's emotional maturity and his ability to control himself? Is it not possible for someone to be able to reason about their behaviour in the minimal M'Naghten sense without being in the full sense a rational agent?

Lord Devlin says that reason alone is the test of responsibility because it gives us 'sovereignty over animate and inanimate things'. It is not clear why such ascendancy, even if accepted, should be a title to legal responsibility. Perhaps he has in mind sovereignty not over this or that aspect of creation, but over oneself: reason is a sufficient ground for attributing responsibility because reason of itself explains personal autonomy. But it is very questionable whether we can analyse the notion of self-rule, which is what autonomy means, simply in terms of reasoning power. People may fail to govern themselves not only through an inability to understand something about their behaviour, but by an inability to align their behaviour with what they do understand. Self-government applies to the whole personality, not to the intellect alone.

Reflections such as these, led to the Rules being widely criticised. They were thought to be too narrowly cognitive in their formulation, with the result that many defendants who ought to have received some protection from the rigours of the law, because of their mental state, were going unprotected. In cases of murder, where the death penalty was in force, this was felt to be intolerable. In response to growing pressure, the new defence of diminished responsibility was introduced. The purpose of section 2 is to allow a defence on the grounds of mental affliction which is less than insanity as legally defined. The courts have consequently interpreted 'abnormality of mind' in a broad sense which covers any abnormality of reason, will or emotion. It is not only a failure of understanding or knowledge which is to count, but any psychological disorder.

It is not disputed that mental abnormality is to be distinguished from legal insanity and in practice the plea of diminished responsibility has virtually displaced the insanity plea. Yet the two continue to be confused. Seymour Spencer (Craft, 1984, pp. 106-13) has given a detailed account of how the defence failed to change gear from 'schizophrenia or nothing' to mental abnormality in the Sutcliffe trial after the plea of diminished responsibility had been rejected by the judge. The defence and the prosecution had presented a united front on the basis of a diagnosis of schizophrenia. The judge insisted that the issue be tried, at which point the issue should have been no longer the correctness of this or that diagnosis, but mental abnormality.

In coming to understand what the law means by abnormality of mind, we must first take note that the law is concerned with psychological states and abilities, not with brain function. No doubt we are not to attribute to the law a philosophical opinion on how mind and brain relate. Nonetheless, in questions of insanity and diminished responsibility, courts concern themselves directly with the psychological aspects of personal abilities and states of mind, and only indirectly with neurological diseases in so far as they are evidence for the impairment of psychological abilities.

Lord Devlin ruled in 1957:

> the law is not concerned with the brain but with the mind, in the sense that 'mind' is ordinarily used, the mental faculties of reason, memory and understanding...the condition of the brain is irrelevant...
>
> (Smith and Hogan, 1973, p. 135)

This would not, of course, prevent neurological evidence being introduced. It could provide grounds for attributing mental abnormality to the accused. But it remains the psychological abnormality, and not neurological disease or damage, that supplies the legal basis for any defence.

The second point to notice is that while it is the psychological state of the accused which constitutes the basis for the defence, the Act is itself generous in the different causes that it envisages may produce the relevant states of mind. The Privy Council has ruled that it is not necessary to tie abnormality of mind into the generally recognised types of insanity. This matters because it means that the abnormality of mind that the law is concerned with is recognizable not only by experts using clinical means. It is a matter for the jury:

> Whether the accused was at the time of the killing suffering from any 'abnormality of mind' in the broad sense...is a question for the jury. On this question medical evidence is no doubt of importance, but the jury are entitled to take into consideration all the evidence, including the acts or statements of the accused and his demeanour. They are not bound to accept the medical

> evidence if there is other material before them which, in their
> good judgement, conflicts with it and outweighs it.
>
> (Elliott and Wood, 1974, p. 340)

It is worth stressing this point. A heavy burden is placed on
the jury from the very beginning of the line of thought that is
supposed to issue in a verdict. Here the jury is required to
decide whether the accused is suffering from abnormality of
mind. Perhaps the heaviness of the burden is one reason why
juries are in the majority of cases not allowed to shoulder it.
Susanne Dell (1982), in her analysis of how section 2 works in
practice, points out :

> ...how rare jury trial is in these cases: 80 per cent are dealt with
> by guilt pleas. When the prosecution does challenge the
> defence, the defence is quite likely to fail: of 28 cases where
> this happened 18 (64 per cent) resulted in murder convictions.

Whatever happens in practice, the only issue that is reserved
to expert witnesses is 'the aetiology of the abnormality'. Psychiatrists may speak authoritatively about mental disease, its
origins and its progression. But whether the defendant exhibits
abnormality of mind, and in particular the extent to which he
exhibits abnormality of mind, is a question which the jury alone
may decide.

These questions of who decides what, are not merely
technical or procedural matters. They reveal what the Act
assumes about the nature of the issues before the court. The
purpose of the Act is to afford a defence which is not based on
insanity either legally or clinically defined. It would be clearly
fatuous to construct such a defence and then reserve the central
issues to legal or clinical experts. The states of mind which are
crucial to the verdict are thought to be determinable by the
common sense judgement and worldly experience of jurors.

Sometimes, as in the judgement we have been quoting, the
reservation of these matters to the jury is grudging. The
suggestion is that one would like a scientific decision at this
point. But since, in our present state of knowledge, the issue
is not scientifically decidable, the only recourse is to the instinct
of the jury. In other judgements, however, more positive

reasons have been given. For example, in the cases we are considering the best evidence that the psychiatrist has on which to base his diagnosis is usually derived from interviews with the accused. The reliability of that evidence is frequently the issue at stake. This does not mean that such evidence is 'from the legal point of view, intrinsically unsatisfactory' as Anthony Storr has suggested (Masters, 1986, p. 320). It means only that what the defendant says about himself, even when mediated through psychiatrists' diagnoses, remains questionable. The credibility of the witness does not cease to be an issue for the jury and suddenly become a medical issue, simply because the statements were elicited by a psychiatrist in a clincial situation. The evidence needs to be supported and tested.

degree of abnormality of mind
Once the jury are satisfied that the defendant exhibits abnormality of mind, 'the crucial question nonetheless arises: was the abnormality such as substantially impaired his mental responsibility for his acts' (Elliott and Wood, 1974, p. 340). The implications of this question are that there are degrees of abnormality of mind, and degrees of mental responsibility, and that the more abnormal the less responsible.

How is the degree of abnormality to be determined? One approach that is not acceptable is to decide the degree of seriousness of abnormality by reference to the degree of impairment of responsibility. Such an approach is revealed in the following exchange between a doctor and a judge in a case in 1961:

> Question: I notice you keep saying, doctor, 'any serious mental illness': would you like to explain that to us? Answer: Well, in the legal sense when I say 'serious mental illness' I mean the type of mental illness which would substantially diminish the responsibility for his actions.
> (R. v. Rose (1961) A.C. 496; (1961) 1 All E.R. 859)

The trouble with this answer is that it implies one of two interpretations neither of which is compatible with the law. If the seriousness of mental abnormality is to be determined by a prior decision about responsibility, the issue of responsibility would be incorporated into the psychiatrist's diagnosis of mental illness. The other alternative is that given a certain medical diagnosis, the issue of responsibility would follow as a matter of legal definition. In either case, the issue of responsibility would be removed from the jury. On the first interpretation, responsibility becomes a matter for the psychiatrists. On the second, it becomes a matter of legal definition. Both outcomes run directly counter to the intention of the Act which is that questions concerning the responsibility of the defendant are substantial issues which should go to the jury for decision.

It may be that the degree of abnormality required by the section ought to be interpreted in quite casual terms. The trial judge in R. v. Walden (1959) found admirably straightforward terms in which to express the matter before the jury:

> There are some cases, you may think, where a man has nearly got to that condition but not quite, where he is wandering on the borderline between being insane and sane; where you can say to yourself, 'Well, really, it may be he is not insane, but he is on the borderline, poor fellow. He is not really fully responsible for what he has done.' Now, you may think, and it is entirely a matter for you, that that is what is meant by those words in the Act of Parliament, 'such abnormality as substantially impairs his mental responsibility'.
>
> (Elliott and Wood, 1974, p. 336)

This interpretation has the advantage of retaining the idea that abnormality and responsibility have degrees, while discouraging the suggestion that either of them, or the relationship between them, can be quantified.

Another important feature of this judgement is that it does not rely on establishing a strong causal link between abnormality of mind and responsibility. There are good reasons to believe that an empirical causal connection between the two is in principle unattainable. Whatever the theoretical difficulties, the practical upshot of insisting on causal links either between psychological abnormality and responsibility or between psychological states and the particular crimes themselves is to make the law very nearly unusable.

The judge in the Sutcliffe trial demanded that the jury satisfy themselves that, at the time of each killing, Sutcliffe was acting under the delusion that he had received a direct command from God and in the belief that his victim was a prostitute. This is a direction which is designed to make the manslaughter verdict extremely difficult to arrive at. How could the jury come to such a retrospective decision about each case, some of which had occurred many years previously? Despite this and other cases, the law has in fact moved away from an interpetation that requires a strong causal link between the particular crimes and the abiding states of mind.

One way of interpreting the move away from strict causal connections is to argue that the sorts of mental affliction which the Homicide Act envisages, are such that there is a conceptual, and not causal, link between the two. This line of argument has the disadvantage of upsetting the basic analogy between physical and mental disease which maintains the distinction between the disease and its symptoms. If there is a conceptual connection between psychopathy and antisocial behaviour, then there is no question of having to establish a causal link between the two.

The price of avoiding the need to make the causal connection between mental affliction and behaviour is that one surrenders the notion of a mental disease which is diagnosable independently of the obnoxious conduct with which it is associated. This may be too high a price to pay. If the idea of a separately diagnosable mental disease is abandoned, then so is the main reason for thinking of the accused's mental state as a mitigating or excusing factor. If one thinks of the accused's behaviour in pathological terms, one is thinking of it as caused in him, in a way closely analogous to the way the symptoms of a physical disease are caused in the patient. The conclusion, of course, is that the accused is no more responsible for his behaviour than patients are for their symptoms.

An alternative strategy is that in the place of a demand for a strong causal connection between the alleged mental disorder and the crime, there should be a presumption that severe mental disorder affects the whole personality and, therefore, responsibility. This has the advantage of retaining the division between psychological assessment and the attribution of responsibility, while softening the requirement that each crime be causally connected with a diagnosable mental condition.

The phrase 'substantially impairs his mental responsibility' is the least satisfactory part of the Act. Alternatives have been suggested. In 1975 the Butler Report suggested the following formulation:

> Where a person kills...he shall not be convicted of murder if there is medical or other evidence that he was suffering from a form of mental disorder as defined in section 4 of the MHA 1959, and if, in the opinion of the jury, the mental disorder was such as to be an extenuating circumstance which ought to reduce the offence to manslaughter.
>
> (1975, Cmnd. 6244, §19.17, p. 247)

The minimum the law requires is that the defendant be shown on the balance of probabilities to be suffering from serious mental abnormality that bears directly on the offences for which he is charged.

mental responsibility

As the focus shifts from abnormality of mind to mental responsibility, one judgement is especially useful in interpreting these undefined categories. In reducing a murder verdict to one of manslaughter, the Court of Appeal made the following remark:

> the Chief Justice...said: 'Do you think that he did that under the influence of this diminished responsibility, or do you think that he knew just exactly what he was doing? Did he intend to do it? If so murder; if not, manslaughter.'
>
> This was a misdirection. A man may know what he is doing and intend to do it and yet suffer from such abnormality of mind as substantially impairs his mental responsibility.
>
> (R. v .Rose (1961) A.C. 496; (1961) 1 All E.R. 859)

In reversing the verdict, the Appeal Court was reaffirming the fundamental point that diminished responsibility is not to be restricted to cognitive considerations. But the judgement also makes clear that over and above any assessment of what the accused knew and intended, there remains a question of whether he was responsible for what he knowingly and intentionally did. When the jury have satisfied themselves that they know the relevant states of mind, the beliefs and the intentions of the accused, they must go on to decide whether this person is to be held fully responsible for his or her actions.

The law on diminished responsibility allows us to decide to withhold full responsibility on psychological grounds. It does not require us to discern lack of responsibility in the psychological make-up of the accused.

There is a strong distinction between legal insanity and diminished responsibility at this point. Insanity is a defence because, not knowing what he is doing or not knowing the moral nature of his act, the insane person is incapable of forming the intentions or having the beliefs that are required for unlawful killing. He has not the *mens rea* for any offence. *Mens rea* is the legal term which refers to the varying mental states that are required for one to be guilty of a particular crime. Almost all acts which are accounted crimes must be accompanied by specified mental states. The legally insane cannot be guilty of these crimes because the actions along with the required mental component, objectively described, cannot be attributed to them. Consequently if the action is not attributable, the issue of responsibility for the action does not even arise. For this reason, insanity is a total defence. An insane person is an innocent person, who has nothing to answer for.

In the case of diminished responsibility, the accused may well meet the requirements of *mens rea*. Therefore the action proscribed by the law is certainly his action. Yet the Homicide Act allows for the possibility that he be held less than fully responsible for his actions, including the mental acts involved in intending to kill. This is a unique moment in English law. Normally, the law presumes that all sane defendants are responsible. But in the case of murder, the jury may be required to consider withholding full responsibility for criminal acts from a person, who is psychologically abnormal but not legally insane.

Whether a person is insane or not is a psychological fact about them. It is a matter of fact which can be ascertained by psychiatric experts. Some psychiatrists are prepared to deny this objective interpretation of insanity. This is an important matter, which affects the assessment of psychiatry as a science. It is also bound to raise questions about the position of expert witness that psychiatrists are given in courts of law. It does not, however, threaten directly the views proposed here. Those who think that insanity is a status decision rather than an objective diagnosis will tend to assimilate the decisions about insanity to the ascription of responsibility. This does not fit the usual assumption, that a psychiatric diagnosis can be kept separate from the moral issues that permeate decisions about responsibility. But it is only if the assimilation is taken in the opposite direction, whereby the ascription of responsibility is thought of as psychiatric diagnosis, that the fundamental assumptions of the law and of the argument here would be threatened.

The identification of responsibility or its absence with a psychological state or capacity would be such a threat. We shall argue, in the next chapter, that whether or not a person is responsible is not a psychological fact about them. It is a matter of the quality of the relationships into which they enter.

All of this is built into English law and into all legal systems that regard responsibility as a substantial jury issue, depending on, but not the same as, psychological assessment.

the verdict
The jury must choose between murder and manslaughter. Manslaughter is the lesser verdict. However diminished responsibility is a unique defence, and the verdict which follows on it shares its unusual characteristics. The purpose of the defence is to gain a conviction to a lesser charge and to attract a more lenient sentence. There are many types of cases which seek the protection of diminished responsibility, of which this is straightforwardly true, for example mercy killing, or crimes of passion committed in a state of depression. In such cases, the logic of the defence follows the usual pattern of excuses with

which the law is normally concerned. Excuses in general have the effect of making the crime less serious than would otherwise be the case or of distancing, to some degree, the criminal from his act. An excuse says: look at the crime from this point of view and it will not appear so bad; or, take into account this fact about the accused and you will feel less inclined to deal harshly with him. Ultimately, excuses are intended to produce at least a partial rehabilitation of the offender in the eyes of the court. Look at it this way, take this into consideration and you won't think he is such a bad chap after all.

This does not seem, however, to be the inspiration behind the defence of diminished responsibility when it is made on behalf of psychopathic killers. The mental abnormality of the accused and his consequent lack of responsibility need not incline the court to take the crimes less seriously or to find some mitigating circumstance that will make the accused appear in a more favourable light. The more one learns about the criminal acts the more brutal they may appear, and the deeper one's insight into the character of the accused the more malicious and depraved he may reveal himself to be.

The anomaly is that the defence in such cases aims at a reduction of the verdict without in the normal sense being a mitigation. This situation is reflected in the sentences that are passed. All persons convicted of murder receive the statutory sentence of life imprisonment. It by no means follows that were a murder charge to be reduced to manslaughter that a more lenient sentence would be imposed.

This peculiarity explains much of the criticism of this aspect of homicide law. Mr Justice Salmon observed of one such criminal:

> ...this man has always committed crimes of violence...These are now invoked in his favour to persuade you, as a jury, that the man is not really responsible for his actions.
>
> (Wootton, 1960, p. 234)

Baroness Wootton, an energetic opponent of the plea of diminished responsibility, enjoyed drawing the conclusion 'The worse your conduct the better your chance' (Wootton, 1960, p. 234).

The judge's remarks bring out the fact that it is only in an odd sense that a man's career of violence can be cited *in his favour*.

It is not just legal experts who have difficulty in accepting the logic of the defence. Much of the popular opposition to it springs from the perception that manslaughter due to diminished responsibility amounts in some sense to letting the criminal off. This feeling persists even though the public knows that such criminals are not treated less severely, than if they had been convicted of murder. David Yallop said of Peter Sutcliffe:

> I do not believe that this man is insane or that he can get off the hook by accepting any one of the vast number of psychiatric labels that have been fastened upon him.
>
> (Yallop, 1981, p. 303)

There are so many hooks in Peter Sutcliffe, and will be until the day he dies, that the issue of letting him off does not, in any substantial sense, even arise.

The implication of section 2 of the Homicide Act is that a person who is legally sane may be less than fully responsible for his criminal acts; it does not follow from the absence of full responsibility that the crimes are less iniquitous, the states of mind he manifests less contemptible or the criminal more lovable.

The assumption that any manslaughter verdict implies a less nasty crime than any murder verdict is suggested by the normal structure of the law:

> Since murder and manslaughter have been distinguished it has always been true to say that the latter, although blameworthy, is a less heinous kind of homicide than the former.
>
> (Russell, 1964, p. 598)

But the diminished responsibility plea has changed that. As Lord Kilbrandon remarked:

> It is no longer true, if it ever was true, to say that murder, as we now define it, is necessarily the most heinous example of unlawful homicide.
>
> (Butler, 1975, p. 246)

One crime may be more odious or hateful than another though the person who perpetrates the former be less responsible than the one who commits the latter. It is the difficulty of accepting this view that accounts for much of the reluctance to accept diminished responsibility as a defence.

Fingarette and Hasse (1979, p. 285) argue that diminished responsibility must affect the intention of the offender. Consequently 'the psychological intent does not reflect that particular "heinous kind of homicide" which is signalled by the phrase "malice aforethought".' This enables them to preserve the traditional relationship between murder and manslaughter. The word 'heinous', however, is not a legal term of art. Though the self-interested and calculated intention to kill is certainly a form of heinousness, it is not the only form. A less calculated but more brutal killing may well strike us as more detestable. Their line of argument is undermined, in any case, because diminished responsibility does not exclude, as we have seen, the forming of the intention to kill.

This interpretation of the manslaughter verdict in cases of diminished responsibility arises from the attempt to maintain the normal grading of murder and manslaughter. Babuta and Bragard, in their book *Evil*, produce a more contrived misinterpretation of the verdict:

> The case of Peter Sutcliffe...raised the possibility of diminished responsibility as the source of the so-called evil. The implication was that part of the total responsibility might lie elsewhere, in those forces and imperatives that led to the diminishment of Sutcliffe's own personal responsibility. Perhaps the social environment – and that means us – was partly to blame for the Ripper's state of mind and therefore his actions.
>
> (Babuta and Bragard, 1988, pp. 34-6)

There are at least three things seriously wrong with this short passage. Diminished responsibility is, neither in law nor in common sense, a source of anything. The source of Sutcliffe's crimes lay in the desires, violent emotions, thoughts, habitual ways of acting and reacting, in short his whole psychological make-up. Responsibility, diminished or otherwise, is not part of that make-up; responsibility, as we shall discuss in Chapter

3, is not a psychological state.

Secondly, the cautionary 'so-called' in the phrase 'so-called evil' is meant to allow for doubts about the evil of Sutcliffe's actions, if it turns out he was seriously mentally disturbed. But whatever one's opinion as to responsibility, there is no need whatever for hesitancy in characterizing as evil Sutcliffe's actions, his intentions, the desires he was satisfying and the emotions that drove him; in general the depravity of his character.

Finally – and this is the forced misreading of the verdict available according to section 2 of the Homicide Act – the notion of diminished responsibility does not imply that part of the total responsibility has migrated to some other place. Conservation of responsibility is not a principle of the moral universe. This is important in practice. For there is nothing more designed to close people's minds to the possibility that killers, such as Sutcliffe, ought to be treated differently from normal offenders than the suggestion that the real responsibility lies with someone else.

The essential structure of English law, as we have seen, is formed by the idea that personal responsibility can be diminished because of the psychological abnormality of the offender, and consequently a verdict different from murder ought to be available to mark this special status. Different legal systems have different ways of accommodating these considerations, but it is interesting to see how closely they in fact relate. It is, of course, possible to argue that this or that formulation of the law captures best the commitments that these fundamental notions embody. But there is no easy way of escaping the structure altogether. Even radical solutions, such as the Californian split trial procedure, deal in the same currency. As do systems that reserve the issues of responsibility to the sentencing authorities, although they deny that the courtroom is the place for the transactions to be negotiated.

Most commentators are critical of the law. Recalling its origins in a strategy to avoid a particular sentence, first death and then life imprisonment, they look forward to a time when the removal of the statutory sentence for murder will finally do away with any residual purpose the category of diminished responsibility may have. They believe the present formulation of the law, and perhaps any formulation, requires that impossible questions be placed before the jury. The suggestion here is that the questions the jury must answer are indeed difficult, but not because of the perversity of the law. The difficulty lies in the character of the defendant. The only way of avoiding the difficulty would be to refuse to face up to the enigmas of the psychopathic character. The current law attempts to do this, by means of a decision process that has three elements, mental abnormality, mental responsibility, and criminal liability. It is just possible that by a happy chance the law has arrived at a structure that mirrors reality tolerably well, and that any suggested simplification could only be adopted at the price of distortion.

When the law is applied to psychopathic killers the question becomes: what is it about the psychopath, if anything, which indicates that he is mentally abnormal to such an extent that he can be held only partially responsible for his criminal acts? Before answering this question, it is necessary to be as clear as possible about the concept of responsibility. For part of the difficulty may lie not in the enigmatic character of the psychopath but in the notion of responsibility. Responsibility therefore is the topic of our next chapter.

notes

Two of the jurists mentioned in this chapter were the leading figures in the most important public dispute concerning society and the law that has taken place in Britain in recent times. The distinguished judge **Lord Devlin**, b. 1905, published *The Enforcement of Morals* in 1959. This sparked off a controversy with the legal philosopher **H.L.A. Hart**, b. 1907. In 1963 he published *Law, Liberty and Morality*, which was in part a reply to Lord Devlin. Their disagreement concerned the extent to which the law ought to be used to enforce the accepted moral standards of society.

A third important participant in public controversy has been referred to in this chapter, **Barbara Wootton**, Baroness Wootton of Abinger, b. 1897. She is a distinguished social scientist and economist, a prolific writer and over many decades a tireless advocate of legal and penal reform.

The legal textbooks from which most of the references to English law in this chapter have been drawn are:

Elliott, D.W. and Wood, J.C., 1974, *A Casebook of Criminal Law*, 3rd. Ed., (London, Sweet and Maxwell).

Smith, J.C. and Hogan, B., 1973, *Criminal Law*, 3rd. Ed. (London, Butterworths).

Other works referred to:

Babuta, Subniv and Bragard, Jean-Claude, 1988, *Evil* (London, George Weidenfeld and Nicolson).

(Butler Report), 1975, Home Office DHSS, Report of the Committee on Mentally Abnormal Offenders, Cmnd. 6244 (London, HMSO).

Dell, Susanne, 1982, 'Diminished Responsibility Reconsidered', *CLR*, pp. 809-18.

Fingarette, H. and Hasse, A., 1979, *Mental Disabilities and Criminal Responsibility* (London, Berkeley, University of Chicago Press).

Holmes, Ronald M. and De Burger, James, 1988, *Serial Murder* (Newbury Park, Sage Publications).

Masters, Brian, 1986, *Killing for Company* (London, Cornet).

Russell, F., 1964, *Russell on Crime*, vol. 1, 12th Ed. by J.W. Cecil Turner (London, Stevens).

Spencer Seymour, 'Homicide, Mental Abnormality and Offence' in Craft, Michael and Ann, 1984, *Mentally Abnormal Offenders* (London, Bailliere Tindall) pp. 106-13.

Wootton of Abinger, Lady, 1960, 'Diminished Responsibility: A Layman's View', *LQR*, vol 76, pp. 224-39.

Yallop, David, 1981, *Deliver Us From Evil* (London, Macdonald Futura Publishers).

3: responsibility

ways of being responsible
A bar sign which hangs in The Tap and Spile reads, 'I have a responsible job round here. If anything goes wrong, I'm responsible.' There is more than one sense of the word 'responsible'.

In one sense of the term, responsibility refers to nothing more than causality, for example, 'the flood, not the earthquake, was responsible for the high mortality'. In another sense, if people are reliable and conscientious, they are said to be responsible. Here it is the name of a particular virtue. In a third sense, it means 'bound to fulfil or fit to undertake specified duties'. This is the sense in which the bar staff are said to have responsible jobs. The implied complaint in The Tap and Spile sign is that 'I have a job with onerous responsibilities. And if anything goes wrong, I get the blame.' The staff would not be blamed, not at least with any justification, were they not in the first place answerable, liable, and accountable if things go wrong. Using the word in this final sense, we say such things as:

The President is responsible for the sorry state of the nation.

Minister X is responsible to Parliament.

Mrs Y is responsible for the damage caused by her child, Master Y.

Miss Z is old enough to be responsible for cleaning her own football boots.

Reckless sailors, who get into difficulties at sea, are responsible for their own plight; they ought, therefore, to be liable for the expenses incurred in rescuing them.

35

The BMA is responsible for enforcing a code of conduct on medical practitioners.

responsibility is not a psychological concept

In the previous chapter it was pointed out that the law does not consider the decision about responsibility to be a psychological matter, even when the crucial evidence is psychological. The above examples conform to this view. For in none of them does responsibility refer to a psychological state. In the political examples, responsibility goes with the job, rather than with any particular attitude of mind. Mrs Y may have been asleep when Master Y broke the window. It is the age of Miss Z that is the basis of the responsibility claim in her case. Indeed, the attribution of responsibility may be made not because the person is in certain psychological states, but because one wishes, among other things, to encourage certain psychological states. In the case of the foolhardy sailors, the suggestion is not that they have had any particular experiences, even though recklessness may involve characteristic states of mind. Finally, when one places the onus of medical discipline on the BMA, one does not thereby attribute psychological states to the institution.

Yet the temptation to think of responsibility as a complex psychological state remains strong. H.L.A. Hart, who begins from responsibility in the sense of legal status, falls back on the supposed psychological sense when the issue of punishment is not in question.

> ...[responsibility for his actions] may be used where no particular question of blame or punishment is in issue and it is then used simply to describe a person's psychological condition.
> (Hart, 1967, p. 360)

Hart refers to this species of responsibility as 'capacity responsibility'. He seems unworried by the thought that a simple description of a person's psychological capacities could be equivalent to an attribution of responsibility.

Why are we inclined to think that responsibility is a psychological state? One reason is that we confuse the psychological criteria which are sometimes the bases on which the ascription of responsibility is made, with responsibility itself. In many cases, though not all, we decide issues of responsibility on the grounds of what the person knew, or what they intended, or what their emotional state was. Even in these cases, however, believing that someone is responsible is not believing this or that about their mental states, but believing that they are answerable for what they have done.

Another reason for thinking that responsibility must ultimately be a psychological state is that while many types of responsibility are unmistakably matters of social relationships and social status, moral responsibility is intensely personal and, as such, seems to belong to individuals in themselves alone. Whether Minister X is responsible for the Navy or Public Health depends on cabinet appointments. Whether he is morally responsible for his own actions depends on nothing of that sort. It is only in the public arena that we can be financially or legally responsible, but moral responsibility belongs in the inner tribunal of conscience. This idea gets expressed in the images of a natural order of justice to which we belong by birth, or the Kingdom of God, of which we are all citizens by redemption.

Moral responsibility and criminal or financial liability differ in obvious and important ways. A way in which they do *not* differ is in one being a form of accountability while the other is a sort of psychological state or frame of mind. They are all forms of responsibility, i.e. they are all forms of accountability. In his book *Rights and Persons*, the philosopher A.I. Melden worries about the phrase 'responsible parents'. To whom are responsible parents accountable? To their infant children? To their future grown-up children? Melden is right to be concerned. If 'responsible' in the phrase 'responsible parents' is taken in the sense of accountable, and not in the sense of dutiful or conscientious, there must be someone or something to which they are responsible. There is no such thing as being accountable – period. One is answerable for certain actions or events, in a particular context, to some person, or group or institution. Different sorts of responsibility, financial, legal, political, or moral, depend on the different things one may be responsible for, to whom, and in what contexts. Moral responsibility differs from other sorts of responsibility in a variety of ways. We are right to think of it as, in some sense, the most intimate sort of responsibility, the most inalienable, and the most important. But it is no less a social concept than any other sort of responsibility.

A third consideration which leads to the separation of moral from other sorts of responsibility is that morality tends to reject parochial or accidental features as they become recognised as such. This gives the illusion that there is an inner core of responsibility which will be revealed when the social and adventitious aspects of our lives are stripped away. There is something right and something wrong about this. Morality does move away from external observances to intentions and motives. It does slowly separate itself from custom and tradition. The move is from the morally accidental to the morally essential. This moral evolution does not need to be mirrored by a psychological shift towards inner states. If responsibility is thought to be a quality of a person's soul, then ascribing responsibility becomes an 'appalling problem' because, as Lady Wootton put it,

> the evidence lies buried in another man's conscience, into which no human being can enter.
>
> (Wootton, 1960, p. 232)

In the legal context this presents a serious problem. The jury are thought to be guessing at something which is forever and in principle hidden from them. The accused may know, but he is either silent or untrustworthy. In any case, if one believes that responsibility lies in a person's soul, one must go the whole hog, and believe it lies in the very depths of the soul, because personal responsibility must be located at the core of personality, and not be passing or variable, like a mood or emotion. The possibility then arises that responsibility is inaccessible to the accused himself.

Being uncertain about one's own responsibility is not only a theoretical possibility, but a common and painful reality. Nigel Balchin remarks about confused old ladies attempting to

co-operate with seventeenth century British courts in ensuring
their own condemnation as witches:

> ...they were pathetically certain that they had done something
> wrong because so many gentlemen appeared to think so; but
> had difficulty in understanding what it was.
>
> (Balchin, 1950, p. 72)

Baronness Wootton draws the obvious conclusion that if the
jury cannot know, and the accused himself may well not know,
then there is only one person who could know:

> Behaviour is observable: culpability, I submit, is not – unless
> by God.
>
> (Wootton, 1960, p. 235)

These difficulties about knowing when people are responsible
for their actions arise from thinking of responsibility as an
especially deeply buried psychological fact. If these difficulties
are genuine, they apply not just to the psychopath, but to us
all. We should allow ourselves to be impressed by the contrast
between the alleged theoretical difficulties and the apparent
ease with which we ascribe and accept responsibility in our
everyday lives.

To deny that responsibility is an inner state is not to deny
the power and the beauty of the image of the 'moral law within'.
It is, however, only an image, an image which distorts, if it
encourages the view that responsibility is a matter of psychological state rather than of social relations.

responsibility and voluntariness

In an immensely influential chapter in the *Nicomachean Ethics*
Aristotle considers the issue of responsibility in his discussion
of the conditions of voluntary action. A voluntary action is one
'of which the originating cause lies in the agent himself, who
knows the particular circumstances of his action'; an
involuntary action, on the other hand, is one done 'under
compulsion or as a result of ignorance' (Aristotle, 1984, p.
115). The details of his account need not concern us here.
Many of the points he makes have become so much part of our
commonsense view that they sound platitudinous.

An implication of running together the accounts of voluntary action and of responsibility is that there does not seem to be room for the question: why should we hold someone responsible for their voluntary actions? If, as a matter of definition, one is responsible for all one's voluntary actions and only one's voluntary actions, there is no further, substantial question about the link between voluntariness and responsibility. A number of reasons suggest that it is important to allow the question. The main one is to keep psychological and forensic concepts separate. If voluntariness is a matter of belief and desire, and if responsibility were the same as voluntariness, then responsibility would consist in those psychological states that go to make up the voluntariness of action.

A second reason for maintaining a distinction between voluntary actions and actions for which the agent is responsible is that we may want to attribute voluntariness to the impaired and to the immature, and even to animals, without holding them responsible for their behaviour. Aristotle allows for this:

> Now choice is clearly a voluntary thing, but the two words have not the same connotation: that of 'voluntary' is wider; for both children and animals have a share in voluntary action, but not in choice; and we call actions done on the spur of the moment voluntary, but not the result of choice.
>
> (Aristotle, 1984, p. 116)

Voluntariness comes down to something close to spontaneity and appropriate belief. These factors can surely be attributed to the behaviour of types of humans and to non-humans about whom the question of responsibility remains to be answered. Children and animals sometimes act voluntarily and sometimes not. The difference between voluntary actions and those done under compulsion or in ignorance is observable in behaviour. It is often immediately obvious. The child being dragged into the supermarket is being compelled. The dog who leaps enthusiastically into the sea to retrieve the stick jumps in voluntarily. In even the most obvious cases, the issue of responsibility nevertheless remains to be settled.

An attempt is sometimes made to preserve the essential connection between responsibility and voluntariness by adding to spontaneity a requirement that animals and some human beings may not be able to meet. Aristotle introduces the element of rational choice. Contemporary philosophers discuss the various interpretations of a stronger sense of freedom than simple voluntariness namely, the sense in which it is said of people that they 'could have done otherwise'. In both cases a sensible question remains. Why should we hold someone responsible for what they do as the result of a deliberate rational choice? Why should we hold someone responsible for their action, given that they could have done otherwise? In the latter case a special problem presents itself. It has often been pointed out that there is a difficulty in ever establishing the truth of the statement, 'he could have done other than he did', or its opposite 'he could not have done other than he did'. It is this difficulty which accounts for the law's reluctance to accept 'irresistible impulse' as a ground for a defence in criminal matters. As Lord Parker said in the Byrne case:

> ...in a case where the abnormality of mind is one which affects the accused's self-control the step between 'he did not resist his impulse' and 'he could not resist his impulse', is, as the evidence in this case shows, one which is incapable of scientific proof.

> (Elliott and Wood, 1974, p. 340)

If voluntariness is to continue to be represented as an empirical psychological concept, the agent's ability to have done otherwise must be established on the basis of further empirical data, i.e. it is to be established on the same sort of evidence which is used to establish spontaneity. If, on the other hand, the ability to do otherwise is not thought of as a quality of the agent which could be established empirically, the notion of voluntariness, which includes the idea of such an ability, can no longer be attributable on the sort of psychological evidence which was sufficient to establish spontaneity.

The question may be reversed: why should we not hold someone responsible for their voluntary actions? The implication of the question is that one needs a special reason *not* to move from voluntariness to responsibility, rather than extra consideration to make the move. In standard cases, this may well be true. There is normally no reason why we should not hold a person responsible for their voluntary actions. If their action was voluntary, that is all we need to know. But this does not close the gap between the psychological concept of voluntariness and the social concept of responsibility. Rather it should draw our attention to the complicated assumptions that lie behind the decision about responsibility. Given we are dealing with a reasonably sane, reasonably adult, reasonably unimpaired member of the relevant community, then once the issue of voluntariness has been decided, the conclusion about responsibility may be drawn without further ado. The trouble is that difficult cases of responsibility tend to call in question those very assumptions that normally lie quietly in the background.

The identification of responsibility with voluntariness tends to displace the various discussions that concern responsibility with the single, though perplexing debate about determinism which sees all events, including those that constitute human action, as absolutely dependent upon their causes, so that whatever happens, including whatever people are said to *do,* happens inevitably. Defending responsibility is easily taken to be the same task as attacking determinism.

The question of determinism is one of the most abstract and metaphysical of philosophical questions; the issues of responsibility are among the most substantial matters of human life. When the two problems are virtually identified it leads to the distortion of the former and to the impoverishment of the latter. The former is confused by loyalty towards or suspicion of human 'freedom and dignity'. The latter is distracted from the study of the behaviour of real people to conceptual analyses about which a main question becomes whether or not the issues at stake have any bearing whatever on our understanding of human behaviour.

In this book we are asking if there are any grounds for treating psychopathic killers *differently* from normal offenders. Clearly, it would not be reasonable to reply: Yes, they ought to be treated differently because their actions are determined, if at the same time one believes that *all* human action is determined. Nor can one reply: No, they ought not to be treated differently because, although their behaviour is determined, all human behaviour is determined and determinism is compatible with holding people responsible. Nor would the position be different if we believed that only psychopathic behaviour was determined, while continuing to believe that issues of responsibility are unaffected by the issue of determinism. Whatever answer we suggest, it must be one that:

(a) distinguishes the psychopathic from the normal;

(b) affects responsibility.

A detailed analysis of determinism, its various interpretations and the different effects it is taken to have on accounts of responsibility, can be found in the companion book in this series, Mark Thornton's *Do We Have Free Will?*

responsibility and punishment

Another attempt to solve the problems connected with the idea of responsibility by assimilating it to a less mysterious notion involves equating responsibility with liability or amenability to punishment.

Moritz Schlick was unimpressed by the apparent intransigence of the problems of freedom and responsibility. He believed that '...it is easy to achieve complete clarity in these matters', provided you identify the question of responsibility with the question 'Who, in a given case is to be punished?':

> The important thing, always, is that the feeling of responsibility means the realisation that one's self, one's own psychic processes, constitute the point at which motives must be applied in order to govern the acts of one's body.
>
> (Schlick, 1962, p. 156)

This strained account of what it is to feel responsible comes from running together his two theses about responsibility. As a subjective experience responsibility is 'simply the consciousness of *freedom*, which is merely the knowledge of having acted of one's *own* desires'. As an objective fact about human behaviour, the acts for which we are responsible are those acts which would be prevented or encouraged, were our desires modified by a punishment system which affected the motives that acted upon us. We are responsible, in a word, for those actions which would be prevented were we to be punished in the event of their occurrence.

This view, that responsibility extends over that range of our behaviour which is modifiable by punishment, is inspired by a no-nonsense, behavioural approach. Schlick believed that the great advantage of his theory, which enabled us to achieve the promised 'complete clarity', was that it identified responsibility with observable changes in behaviour. His account is stringently behavioural in that he interpets responsibility as the capacity for behavioural modification effected by punishments and the threat of punishments that act as motives on 'our psychic processes'.

Anthony Kenny defends another theory which ties responsibility equally tightly into the concept of punishment, but which is not inspired by a commitment to interpret everything we can say about people in terms of observable behaviour. In particular Kenny develops his views in terms of reasons for actions, not motives. He concentrates on the penal system's function of supplying reasons for action and restraint in the form of the threat of punishment, which a normally competent agent can take into account. He does not talk in the quasi-mechanical terms of Schlick's application of motives to a psychic point.

> Once one has set out what is involved in the attribution of *mens rea* (namely, an inquiry into the the agent's reasons for his action) and what is the purpose of punishment (the provisions of reasons for abstaining, through fear, from anti-social action) the connection between *mens rea* and responsibility becomes self-evident: the two concepts fit together like a key and a lock. The connection between the deterrent purpose of punishment and the necessity of *mens rea* if a crime is to be imputed is made *via* the concept of practical reasoning: the attachment of penal sanction to legislation is precisely an attempt to affect the practical reasoning of citizens.
>
> (Kenny, 1978, pp. 79-80)

Kenny believes that responsibility arises when one considers the spectrum of mental states which are covered by the standard considerations of *mens rea*, in the light of a deterrent theory of punishment. 'Responsibility, in the appropriate sense, is liability to punishment' (Kenny, 1978, p. 69). If a law-breaker satisfies the requirements of *mens rea*, nothing more is required for him to be liable to punishment. Consequently; given a proper understanding of the penal system, there are no further considerations relevant to the issue of responsibility than those psychological matters concerning the offender's knowledge and intentions that go to make up *mens rea*.

Kenny's version of deterrence relates to the effect punishment has on the population as a whole. It is not necessary that the criminal be deterred by his punishment, but that the penal system has a desirable effect on the general run of citizens. This leads to the awkward conclusion that someone who is personally unaffected by the threat of punishment is responsible, i.e. becomes liable to punishment, because his fellow citizens are by and large amenable to such pressures. Kenny is unembarrassed by the conclusion that a recidivist ought to be punished even though it is not going to be of any benefit to him, because he does not believe that it is a primary purpose, nor even a necessary condition of justifiable punishment, that it benefit the criminal.

Utilitarians, who are inclined to favour deterrence as the right sort of justification for penal institutions, are often accused of being unable to avoid the conclusion that one should punish the innocent if thereby one promotes the general welfare. Of course, Kenny is not saying that. He does say, however, that one can punish law-breakers even though one knows that the punishment is not going to do them the slightest bit of good. It may be argued that to find this a difficulty is to confuse two questions: first, what is the justification of punishment in general? And second, what is the best thing to do with this recalcitrant criminal? But the confusion of these two questions has already occurred when the issue of personal responsibility is tied into the deterrence theory of punishment. Liability to punishment is identified with the responsibility of the criminal and it is justified by the utilitarian consideration that the imposition of punishment (even on the hopelessly recalcitrant) ensures that 'the threat of punishment is not an empty threat' (Kenny, 1978, p. 75). This makes the issue of John Doe's personal responsibility hang on the effectiveness of the threat of punishment on John Doe's neighbours.

This consequence is the result of Kenny's attempt to present the accounts of *mens rea* and of insanity and of diminished responsibility as a seamless robe. He wants insanity and mental abnormality to excuse, in so far as they do, for precisely the same reasons as the complicated and varying considerations that constitute *mens rea*. It seems, however, to be better, though less economical, to interpret insanity and diminished responsibility as different considerations from those psychological matters that effect the criminal liability of the normal offender.

Keeping insanity and abnormality as separate considerations fits in with the general structure of the law. The responsibility of the defendant is assumed. Raising issues of responsibility depends (almost always) on the initiative of the defence, which is not true of *mens rea*, which is as much the concern of the prosecution as of the defence. In relation to homicide, which is our special concern, Kenny's theory cannot represent the intention of the law. As we have seen, according to the Homicide Act, 'mental responsibility' is to be determined prior to the decision about criminal liability, and consequently prior to the decision about punishment. The Act, therefore, presumes there is a separate set of questions about responsibility which ought to be asked prior to the determination of liability to punishment.

For these reasons, Kenny's assimilation of the responsibility issues connected with insanity and mental abnormality to the general considerations of *mens rea* does not seem to reflect the attitude of the law. The approach of Herbert L. Packer seems more accurate when he writes:

> ...the insanity defense is not implied in or intrinsic to the complex of mental element defenses that make up most of the law of culpability. It is an overriding, *sui generis* defense that is concerned not with what the actor did or believed but with what kind of person he is.

(Packer, 1969, p. 135)

The basic reasons, however, for rejecting the identification of responsibility with liability to punishment do not concern law courts. Issues of responsibility occur in personal and domestic relations, where the question of punishment rarely, if ever, arises. Though it is of the first importance to remember that decisions about criminal responsibility lead inexorably to the question of punishment, this does not mean that responsibility changes its nature when it occurs in the legal domain. To ascribe responsibility in any sphere is to hold someone answerable for their behaviour. The question of punishment, if it arises at all, is a new question, and different considerations come to bear.

There is a tactical advantage in keeping a distance between responsibility and punishment. Contemporary theories of punishment are in a state of confusion, while current practices of punishment seem ineffective and uncertain. The sorts of penal programme that characterise modern developed societies are defensible only on the grounds that we cannot think of anything better or organise political support for a more promising policy. Many people are suspicious of the notion of responsibility. They believe it should have no role in penal matters. Often their view is inspired by a low opinion of current penal practices. This lack of faith in our penal institutions reinforces the theoretical prejudice that a defence of responsibility amounts to an apology for vindictiveness. Criticisms that are directed at responsibility are frequently displacements that find a good target when directed at our patently unsatisfactory institutions of punishment.

In such a situation the defenders of responsibility do well to distance themselves from the apologists for the present penal system, if indeed any such apologists can be found. They must insist on the advantages, both for individual maturity and social welfare, of maximising our sense of personal responsibility. The benefits which flow from a developed sense of responsibility are not to be confused with the much less apparent and more questionable advantages that society and individuals may or may not derive from present, or indeed any conceivable, penal practices.

punishment, praise and blame

The contrast of the domestic and the legal may be challenged on the grounds that though formal punishment may not be part of the domestic scene, praise and blame are. Praise and blame are often presented as informal or minimal rewards and punishments. On this view, the conceptual connection between responsibility and punishment, however minor, is retained.

For the argument of this book it is important to resist this suggestion. Praise and blame are direct, personal responses. As are resentment, admiration, envy, contempt and a host of other reactions. Praise and blame are conceptually connected to responsibility. They flow as natural social consequences in situations where there is the possibility of doing well or badly, where people care about the outcome. and where responsibility is attributable. If I insult you, you will resent my words. If you score the winning goal, I will admire you; if you write philosophy books with ease, I will envy you. If you drive too fast, I will blame you. There are occasions where both praise and blame are formalised into a ritual, at which point they may border on rewards and punishments. The recipient of an honorary degree listens while a eulogizing speech is read out by the university's public orator. Blame can be so heavily and persistently laid on that it causes psychological pain or damage which may then be interpeted as a punishment. Nevertheless these borderline cases do not destroy the distinction between social consequences and a system of penalties and rewards.

Treating each other as responsible agents, and the attendant practices of praise and blame, are forms of social competence. Punishing people, at home or abroad, is a matter of policy.

J.S. Mill, in a different context, argues for a similar distinction:

> ...a person may suffer very severe penalties at the hands of others for faults which directly concern only himself; but he suffers these penalties only in so far as they are the natural and, as it were, the spontaneous consequences of the faults themselves, not because they are purposely inflicted on him for the sake of punishment.

(Mill, 1968, p. 134)

We blame persons. Blame is a person-seeking missile. We do not blame, except in an extended sense, habits or emotions or desires. When we blame someone we interact with them.

It is often suggested that parsimonious metaphysics and healthy scepticism come together with enlightened morality to prevent our moral attention reaching to persons themselves. Cautious metaphysics suspects that the *person* as the focus of moral judgements is a fiction. Healthy scepticism doubts whether anyone is in a position to make reliable judgements about the person, even should such an entity exist. Enlightened morality preaches that we should leave people out of it. On the last day God may be in a position to separate the sheep from the goats, but we should accept the advice, 'hate the sin, not the sinner'. As a caution against vindictiveness, who would object? Literally speaking, however, it is nonsense.

J.J.C. Smart has defined blame as grading a person's actions plus an ascription of responsibility, and used this dispassionate understanding to arrive at the conclusion that:

> we should be quite as ready to *grade* a person for his moral qualities as for his non-moral qualities, but we should stop *judging* him. (Unless 'judge' just means 'grade' as in 'judging apples').

(Smart, 1961, p. 306)

The odd thing Smart fails to notice in his determination to be non-judgemental is that grading is a form of judgement, a form of judgement that is consciously striving for objectivity. Blame is a direct censuring of one person by another. Grading is cold, blaming is hot. Blaming people and, in one sense (different from grading), judging people is just what we should do; grading them we ought not to bother about, except on special occasions and then only in regard to certain capacities or achievements. We can leave grading people to examiners, sports coaches and games show hosts. We can manage very well without grading. It is difficult, on the other hand, to conceive of human life without the direct interpersonal relations of which blaming is one example.

responsibility and authority

The decision that faces us is whether the psychopath is responsible for his actions. The argument so far is that responsibility does not refer to any psychological state or set of capacities. Not does it mean voluntariness, nor liability or amenability to punishment. It is a necessary condition of responsible action that the agent have certain cognitive and volitional capacities. But these are not sufficient conditions, so the possibility arises that someone could satisfy them and yet not be responsible. Nor is the crunch question: would the psychopath, or anyone else, benefit from the imposition of punishment? Although if punishment is clearly fatuous, this may be taken as an indication that we have moved from the sphere of responsible behaviour. Questions of responsibility both in law and everyday life precede questions of punishment. The first issue is accountability. Only when that issue is resolved, or when a resolution is assumed, does the question of penalty, if any, arise. The first question is: can the psychopath answer for his actions? Can he give an account of himself? The important requirement is that his answers be authoritative. When President Truman said 'the buck stops here', he wasn't making a disclosure of his psychological state, nor referring to the possibility of impeachment. He was both accepting responsibility for his actions and asserting his authority. The two go together.

Though the psychopath, unlike the legally insane, has the psychological competence to speak up for himself, it is difficult to imagine what he is to say or how he is to comport himself in order that his words should have any authority with us. What threatens the ascription of responsibility in the case of the psychopath is neither cognitive nor executive incompetence but a fundamental lack of authority.

The difficulty we have with the psychopath reaches right through to his status as a person. In this context Jonathan Glover makes some interesting remarks in relation to blame. He is aware of the personal aspect of blame:

> Blame as we know it involves identifying the person who is the object of blame with his intentions, and treating other factors influencing his conduct as external. Even his mental abilities

> are seen as being possessed by the person rather than as being part of the person blamed.
>
> But not all intentions are seen as internal to the person blamed. Sometimes a person's intention is one that he does not identify with, or endorse, and is one he would prefer to be without...
>
> To sum up crudely: for purposes of blame, a person is his intentions, except where his intentions are unalterable.
>
> (Glover, 1970, p. 66)

Glover is right to say that blame, and other concepts of responsibility, search out persons, and that persons, as agents, relate in a special way to their intentions. He is also right to point out that it is not as simple as that. Some intentions are disowned. The trouble we have in understanding the psychopathic killer is that we find it unimaginable that he could endorse the intentions with which he acts. And for ourselves we find it impossible to acknowledge and endorse them in others. Glover goes wrong in identifying the inability to endorse intentions with the inability to change them or with a preference not to have them. The ability to change one's intentions is a psychological capacity, endorsement is a matter of authority.

The psychopath must answer up. Hart makes the following etymological point about responsibility:

> The original of the word answer...was not that of answering questions, but that of answering or rebutting accusations or charges which if established carry liability to punishment or blame or other adverse treatment.
>
> (Hart, 1967, p. 363)

There does not seem to be a conflict between the two interpretations. Rebutting an accusation surely involves answering questions such as: Did you do it? or Why did you do it? To these we may add others, equally obvious, which we are all anxious to ask:

What did you think you were doing?

What excuses can you offer?

What do you think of yourself, given that you have done these things?

How do you expect us to relate to you, given that you have these desires and are driven by these emotions?

How do you relate, even in your imagination, to the people you have injured?

Have you any suggestions for a way back to ordinary human relations after these outrages?

The old idea of 'moral imbecility' suggests that someone could be such an imbecile, though (mysteriously) only in the moral domain, that he is incapable of answering these questions. Such a person may have grave difficulty in answering, or rather in having anything he says accepted as an answer. The difficulty is not physical or psychological. The problem is: given the gravity of the offences, what could count as authoritative answers?

notes

Books and articles referred to in this chapter:

Aristotle, 1984, *Ethics*, trans. J.A.K. Thomson (Harmondsworth, Penguin Books).

Balchin, N., 1950, *The Anatomy of Villiany* (London, Collins).

Elliott, D.W. and Wood, J.C., 1974, *A Casebook of Criminal Law*, 3rd. Ed. (London, Sweet and Maxwell).

Glover, J., 1970, *Responsibility* (London, Routledge and Kegan Paul, N.Y., Humanities Press).

Hart, H.L.A., 1967, 'Varieties of Responsibility', The Law Quarterly Review, vol. 83, pp. 346-64.

Kenny, Anthony, 1978, *Freewill and Responsibility* (London, Routledge and Kegan Paul).

Melden, A.I., 1977, *Rights and Persons* (Berkeley and Los Angelos, University of California Press).

Mill, J.S., 1968, *Utilitarianism, On Liberty and Considerations on Representative Government* (London, Dent).

Packer, Herbert, L., 1969, *The Limits of the Criminal Sanction* (Stanford, California, Stanford University Press).

Schlick, M., 1962, *Problems of Ethics*, tr. David Rynin (N.Y., Dover Publications Inc.).

Smart, J.J.C., 1961, 'Freewill, Praise and Blame', *Mind*, vol. LXX, pp. 291-306.

Wootton of Abinger, Lady, 1960, 'Diminished Responsibility: A Layman's View', *Law Quarterly Review*, vol. 76, pp. 224-39.

4: character and responsibility

what is wrong with psychopaths?
So far the argument has been that the criminal liability of psychopathic killers depends on their personal responsibility for their criminal acts; personal responsibility consists in accountability for one's actions. If the responsibility of psychopaths is in question it must be because their ability to answer up for their crimes is in doubt. Why should this be? Many psychopaths are persons of normal or even above average intelligence. What could it be about them that undermines accountability?

Psychopathic killers are people whose personalities are by common consent unusual, whose desires are aberrant, sometimes wildly so, and who are subject to strong violent emotional pressures. A correspondent to *The Times* (May 26th, 1981), Marion Oerton, observed:

> If the law really treats as sane a man who murders 13 women in the circumstances attending Sutcliffe's crimes, then the law can be described only in Mr. Bumble's immortal phrase.

This commonsense diagnosis of insanity simply on the basis of the crimes themselves is open to a charge of circularity. Baroness Wootton expresses the criticism in the following terms:

> ...just as, in the case of an anti-social act that is said to be due to mental illness, the existence of the illness cannot, without circular argument, be inferred solely from the fact that the act was committed, so also it must not be inferred that an impulse was irresistible merely because it was not resisted. If irresistible impulse or diminished responsibility is to be a valid excuse for anti-social actions, some criterion of irresponsibility must be

found which is independent of the act itself.
(Wootton, 1959, p. 233)

She is right to insist on a criterion for responsibility which is distinct from the bare commission of the crime. But it is not clear in what way the thought behind Marion Oerton's remark is viciously circular. She implies that the crimes are manifestations of a particular character, and that there is something about this character which clearly places the criminal outside the realm of normally responsible people. The argument would be circular if the peculiarity of character were explained by the mere fact that the character gave rise to the crimes. We have to say what dispositions of character, what personality traits, what psychological states provide criteria for the withholding of responsibility.

Before asking what it is about aberrant psychological make-up that could put responsibility in doubt, we should consider in what ways character, which is well within the bands of normality, affects the responsibility of the average person.

the threat of passivity

Character, desire and emotion refer to different aspects of a person's psychological make-up. Different things have to be said about them. Character refers to structural and enduring qualities of the person, whereas desire and emotion are episodic features of a person's experience. However, they have this similarity: they all seem to threaten responsibility for the same broad reason. They all highlight ways in which the person is acted upon, moulded, and consequently, in some way passive. The threat to responsibility arises from the introduction of passivity into the centre of human agency. Our personalities are formed by all sorts of factors outside our own control. We need not take sides in the nature/nurture argument. On any view, our characters are not chosen like shirts or holiday locations, they are the products of genetic inheritance, of culture, of upbringing, of accident. The same factors affect our desires. In this context puberty is an interesting phenomenon. During this exciting and painful phase of life our desires change.

Our characters are not chosen like shirts or holiday locations.

The way we see the world undergoes a fundamental alteration. These changes deeply affect every aspect of our lives. They take place gradually, but not so gradually as to be undetectable. Nor do they take place at a stage of life at which self-awareness is non-existent or minimal, as do the changes in early infancy. They constitute the most dramatic changes in one's character and one's experience of life that one is in a position to oversee. One has to act and react on a stage in which the scenery is being moved. We, the actors, are passive in two respects. We do not choose our new desires. We talk about the 'onset' of puberty. Nor do we, generally speaking, choose when or to what extent we are affected by our desires. As regards emotion, the very word expresses the idea of passivity. The traditional philosophical term for the emotions is the *passions of the soul.* An emotion would not be an emotion unless it moved the one experiencing it.

It is because of the threat that passivity poses, that extreme libertarians, like Sartre, deny the reality of character and reinterpret the phenomena of desire and emotion. What we take to be our characters, which limit our options and shape our behaviour, are in fact alienated decisions. We mistake, he believes, our own decisions for nature-imposed or socially determined structures of personality. Consequently what appear in our immediate experience to be limitations on possible action are self-imposed restrictions.

> For suppose that, like Zola, we showed that the behaviour of these characters was caused by their heredity, or by the action of their environment upon them, or by determining factors, psychic or organic. People would be reassured, they would say, 'You see, that is what we are like, no one can do anything about it.' But the existentialist, when he portrays a coward, shows him as responsible for his cowardice...he has made himself into a coward by his actions.
>
> (Sartre, 1980, pp. 42-3)

Some philosophers who accept the reality of character and who do not share the existentialists' idea of radical freedom, nonetheless read the relationship between character and responsibility in a similar way. To the extent that behaviour is attributable to character it cannot be attributable to persons as moral agents, except in so far as past behaviour makes them responsible for aspects of their own characters. On this view, responsibility for one's own character does not involve the choice of one's character. It is sufficient that past actions, for which one was responsible, mould present dispositions. This is the view of Aristotle:

> 'Well, probably he is the sort of person that doesn't take care.' But people get into this condition through their own fault, by the slackness of their lives; i.e. they makes themselves unjust or licentious by behaving dishonestly or spending their time in drinking and other forms of dissipation; for in every sphere of conduct people develop qualities corresponding to the activities that they pursue. This is evident from the example of people training for any competition or undertaking: they spend all their time exercising. So to be unaware that in every department of conduct moral states are the result of corresponding activities is the mark of a thoroughly unperceptive person.
>
> (Aristotle, 1984, pp. 123-4)

The weakness of the analogy between the way past behaviour moulds character and the way exercises prepare one for an athletic event indicates the weakness of the whole argument. For example, however strong one believes the relationship between pornography and sexual crime to be, one would not say that the man who is perusing a pornographic magazine is training for rape. The relationship between present action and future personality is much less overt than that between a training programme and a coming event. The problem is that the more indirect and insidious, the less predictable the effect becomes. Consequently, the less plausible it is to suggest that one's responsibility for actions that spring from well-established traits of character, is adequately explained in terms of responsibility for past actions.

Aristotle's defence of responsibility – for that is what it means to be – concedes too much. It encourages the belief that in so far as action is attributable to the personality of the agent, to that extent the agent is not responsible. We will try to present an alternative picture of human action which will make this view seem less compelling. Besides this general point, if we explain accountability for actions which are rooted in personality traits in terms of prior responsibility for past action, we don't get what we want, namely responsibility for current action. We are assimilating the relationship of character to action with that of a chemical agent, such as drink or drugs. Those who are so befuddled by drugs that they are incapable of forming the intention required for a criminal act, cannot be responsible for that act as such, although they can be held responsible for taking the drugs and, in varying degrees, for their subsequent behaviour.

It would be paradoxical if the importance of personality in human behaviour were to force us to have recourse to this indirect form of responsibility. For example, those who are convinced that exposure to pornography has a direct causal relationship with sexual crime would not be satisfied if the sexual offender were to be held responsible only for those (perhaps) non-criminal acts in the past which led to his habituation to pornography, and to subsequent crime. It is for his crimes he is to be held responsible.

character and responsibility

As part of his diagnosis of the current state of moral philosophy, Bernard Williams says:

> ...morality is under too much pressure on the subject of the voluntary...
> There is a pressure within [morality] to require a voluntariness that will be total and will cut through character and psychological and social determination, and allocate blame and responsibility on the ultimately fair basis of the agent's own contribution, no more and no less. It is an illusion to suppose that this demand can be met (as opposed to the less ambitious requirements of voluntariness that take character largely as given).

> (Williams, 1985, p. 194)

If moral responsibility is interpreted on the model of criminal liability, i.e. as primarily a concern about retribution for individual acts, a dichotomy opens up between the moral agent and the real, particular person walking down the street. The particular person has a genetic inheritance, a history, an upbringing, all of which seem to complicate the allocation of blame. Fairness requires that we disentangle the contributions of nature and nurture from voluntary action before making moral judgements. What we are left with is the idea of a rational agent, whose behaviour is explained solely in terms of its decisions.

In this way, we generate the concept of the will, which we think of as the executive branch of rationality. The discussion about the responsibility people have for their actions can now be transformed into a discussion about the freedom of the will. A major threat to this freedom will be the other dynamic aspects of the human character, from which we have been concerned to distinguish the will. Desires, emotions, moods, energy, habits and inclinations are thought of as alien forces that are brought to bear on the will, and consequently threaten its freedom. In the normal person these non-rational parts of personality are thought to be under the control of reason, or at most to limit, without destroying, the scope of rational choice. In the abnormal, the suggestion is that the non-rational reigns. The rational agent is overthrown.

The will is made to bear all the moral weight, while the individual person, with a history, an education, and a personality is thought to fall outside the moral domain. This is what fairness seemed to demand in the first place. Our characters are seen as part of the world which stands over against the will. This is the picture that Williams has sketched out. 'The agent's own contribution' is presented as what 'he' has done within the confines set by an alienated character. In the pursuit of fairness, we distinguish what is attributable to the will from everything else. We think of the 'everything else' as whatever the agent has been lumbered with.

The consequence is that we get a purer and purer idea of the moral agent, about whom we can say less and less, and yet who alone is a suitable object of our moral attention. On the other hand, the notion of character tends to expand. The more we know about the patterns of human behaviour, and the more we know about the motivations, conscious and unconscious, that underlie our actions, the thicker our concept of character becomes and the thinner the idea of the will. In this way character draws into itself more and more aspects of human behaviour, while presenting itself as lying outside the sphere of the properly moral.

Correspondingly, the will becomes increasingly other-worldly and mysterious. It is represented as sheer activity, pure spontaneity, caught somehow or other in an alien world, which is, by its very nature, the will's metaphysical dead opposite. There is a split between free will and the recalcitrant world which encompasses everything from mountains and trees to moods, emotions and traits of character. Defending human freedom understood in this sense involves representing people as some- how or other outside of the natural order.

the world and the will
Philosophers intent on defending human freedom have had to explain the relationship between the will and the world. Some have felt compelled to divide the human individual into two component parts, mind and matter, soul and body. This dualism requires an explanation of how the corporeal and the incorporeal can interact. Determinists reject any defence of freedom based on such mysterious interactions. They exploit the inherent irrationality of explaining human action in the world by appealing to a source of transcendent agency. According to them, introducing the will onto the world's stage presents the same difficulties that face the theatrical producer who has to represent Tinkerbell in productions of *Peter Pan*. The theatrical problem is resolved by having pure, ethereal light flitting free among the props and the paint. The determinist's conviction is that however fervently we assert our belief in the fairy of Free Will, the light is doomed to fade and die. Any sort of inter-actionism is bound to introduce passivity into the heart of the will, thus undermining the purity of its activity.

Consequently, when the force of determinism is appreciated, it seems resistible only by the heroic step of removing the will from the world altogether. This step has been taken by many thinkers, particularly those influenced by Kant. The removal may be mystical, as in Wittgenstein's *Tractatus.* Or more brashly romantic, as in existentialism. It may manifest itself methodologically, in e.g. the fact/value distinction, or linguistically, in differences of speech act, e.g. prescription versus description. The purpose is the same in all cases, to keep the world and the will apart. The universe is too small for both of them.

If we wish to avoid these extravagances we have to accept the implication not only that the people are active as well as passive (which no-one would wish to deny) but that their activity is itself moulded by the world of which it is a part. Human beings, unlike God, grow and develop. Their development is subject to all sorts of contingencies outside of their control. Yet their development is genuinely theirs. It is not some sort of accommodation that takes place at the interface of person and environment. It is a moulding of the person and their capacities. John Stuart Mill realised that character is an integral part of human agency and that desires and emotions could not be seen as nothing but 'a peril and a snare':

> A person whose desires and impulses are his own – are the expressions of his own nature, as it has been developed and modified by his own culture – is said to have a character. One whose desires and impulses are not his own, has no character, no more than a steam-engine has a character. If, in addition to being his own, his impulses are strong, and are under the government of a strong will, he has an energetic character.
>
> (Mill, 1968, p. 118)

Talking about the will as a faculty is a traditional and almost unavoidable way of referring to a set of human capacities. That the will itself could be moulded by external contingencies, may seem incoherent. Is not free will precisely the power to act independently of such external factors? This line of thought must be rejected. Its consequence is to deify the human person, and its inspiration is the false idea that any element of passivity in human behaviour is an invasion of anti-will into the heart of the will itself.

The problem is generated when we prefer the fiction of will to the individual person. In pursuit of fairness we abstract from the strengths and weaknesses of the particular person, in search of some inner kernel of personhood. The result is a double distortion of the individual person and of character. In relation to the issue of responsibility, person and character become rivals. What is attributed to persons cannot apply to their characters. Character becomes a suit of armour inside which a person makes increasingly tiny movements in their efforts to act in the world.

This progression of thought reaches back to the beginnings of modern philosophy:

> ...if I examine my memory, or imagination, or any other faculty, I find none which is not very small and limited, and in God immense and infinite. It is will alone that I experience to be so great in me that I conceive the idea of no other as more ample and more extended; so that it is my will principally which tells me that I bear the image and resemblance of God.
>
> (Descartes, 1968, p. 136)

This deification of will is incompatible with acknowledging the genetic endowment of historical individuals, the dispositions which they have acquired on their way through life, and the many other aspects of personality which manifest the fact that their activity depends on interaction with their social and physical environments. The will that we are left with is an abstraction, which, if we insist on imagining it as an existing individual, must be some sort of metaphysically simple creature. The reason why human agency demands character is that human beings are complex and developing creatures acting over time in a complex and changing world. How else could learning and experience be appropriated into the individual organism except through more or less stable, acquired patterns of action and reaction?

We can approach the idea of an agent that had no character by imagining a very simple creature with, let us say, only one desire and one way of satisfying it. During the day it extends its tendrils and during the night it retracts them. All members of the species behave in an identical way. Their behaviour is immune from modification through experience or learning, and they cannot develop habits. We are, nevertheless, not inclined to identify this immunity with freedom. The more traditional candidate for agency without character is found at the other end of the chain of being. God must be thought of similarly as beyond modification. This leaves the ancient problem of how to attribute action to God without assuming that he interacts with his creation. So we may conceive the characterless agent, according to our taste, as god or mollusc, but not, at any rate, as a human being.

emotion and responsibility

Similar problems arise when we consider emotion in relation to responsibility for action. If responsibility is identified with sheer activity, to the extent that our behaviour is affected by our emotional states, we are not responsible. This threat to responsibility extends to virtually all human behaviour, because little or nothing we do is unaffected by emotion, and it clearly encompasses psychopathic behaviour which is characterised by violent and unusual emotional states.

Two illuminating responses to this problem are provided by Descartes and Sartre. Both are anxious to defend human freedom and thereby responsibility. Both see the emotions as jeopardizing that freedom. They react, however, in opposite ways. Descartes saves the integrity of the human will by excluding the emotions from the sphere of the will in so far as he plausibly can. Emotions are physiological disturbances of which we are aware. The will and the emotions act on each other only indirectly. The feeling, which is an awareness of bodily changes, entices the will to act. Providing an incentive is all the motivation that emotion contributes.

Sartre adopts the opposite strategy. He undermines the assault the emotions make against freedom by incorporating the emotions into the dynamism of the will itself. Emotions are alienated decisions which are experienced as passions that affect the will. In fact the emotions are our own, unacknowledged products by which we, having failed to control the world in realistic and practical ways, contrive to mould it to our tastes 'magically'. Emotion transforms the experienced world into a more bearable environment.

> ...the origin of emotion is a spontaneous debasement lived by the consciousness in face of the world. What it is unable to endure in one way it tries to seize in another...
>
> ...the consciousness is caught in its own snare...The consciousness of the emotion is captive, but by this it must not be understood to be fettered by anything whatever outside itself.
>
> (Sartre, 1981, pp. 79-80)

Both Descartes and Sartre go to great lengths, in opposite directions, to ensure that freedom is not imperilled by emotion. In their anxiety, they do not do justice to the complexity of the passivities that emotion involves and they overestimate the ways in which emotion threatens responsibility.

Consider for example: you made me feel nostalgic for Tyneside by singing the Blaydon Races. The first passivity involves my relationship to you. You acted upon me and aroused certain feelings in me. Unless your singing is quite unusually bad, I don't experience this as an imposition. Being open to such influences is part of social competence, not a sort of vulnerability.

What caused my surge of sentiment was the singing of the song. Here the experience of being acted upon can be very strong. I bite my lip and think about London but the tears come to my eyes anyway. The tension I feel is again not one that indicates a threat to freedom. On the contrary, when I *give in* and allow the tears to flow, I may well feel that I have at last overcome my inhibitions, which were limits on freedom, and allowed myself to express my true nature.

The singing alters my view of things. It opens my eyes. Up until that moment I had not realised what a fascinating place Tyneside is. It stimulates my imagination and my memory. I decide, moved by these strong feelings, to write the novel *Growing up on Tyneside* which had only been a dream before.

These are some of the ways in which one is acted upon in an emotional situation. None of them undermine freedom and some of them increase it. It is only when emotions become impediments that a threat occurs. Perhaps when it is my turn to entertain and I rise to sing *Cushie Butterfield*, I am so choked with emotion that I cannot begin. If it is important that I make

my contribution to the Annual Nostalgia Party, this is a
significant failure and I had better acquire some self-control.

The example shows that not all instances of being moved,
even of being deeply moved are instances of being overcome.

the psychopathic personality and responsibility

We have taken character and emotion as instances, one structural and one episodic, of the way in which human action
presumes a context of interaction with other people and the
environment. It is not possible to account for activity without
reference to things undergone, experienced and imposed. Our
suggestion has been that not only are character and emotion
compatible with responsible action, but that in case of human
beings, at any rate, responsible action is impossible without
them.

However, it was not just a mistake to think that there may
be something about the psychopathic personality that raises
the question of responsibility. Whatever it is, it cannot be the
simple fact that the psychopath has definite traits of character,
that he has deeply ingrained habits of thought and behaviour,
or that he is strongly inclined to act the way he does. This is
true of all of us, and if it were not true, a coherent, developing
personal life and a stable, social existence would be impossible.
There must be distinctive features of the characters we cate-
gorize as psychopathic, if their responsibility is to be challenged.

Could, for example, the great pecularity of their depraved
desires provide a ground? It is important to consider desires
because, in the cases we have in mind, they are a crucial
element in the explanation of the depraved behaviour. This is
not always the case. It does not seem true of some of the most
promising candidates for the position of the worst person who
ever lived. Himmler, for example, would be indignant, and
perhaps with justification, if an explanation was offered of his
ghastly career in terms of his succumbing to depraved desires.
But the psychopathic killer may attempt to excuse his crimes
on the grounds that he could not help himself, that he experienced irresistible desires, that his desire to do something was
compulsive or bordered on the compulsive. Equally the

moralist, even if he rejects the attempted exoneration, will appeal to desire in his explanation of the malice of the act: this person gave in to passion.

It is often said that the desires of the psychopath are unintelligible. That such people exist and have those desires is a fact that is brought home to us with depressing regularity. It is surprising that we continue to find something unintelligible about it. Nor is the nature of aberrant desire so disconnected from normal experience that we cannot make head nor tail of it. Yet the feeling persists that there is something deeply irrational about such behaviour and the emotional experience that animates it. The feeling may be misconstrued but it is unlikely to be without any foundation. We can suggest three ways in which grossly aberrant desires may appear incomprehensible and consequently raise difficulties about responsibility.

desires and their objects
Desires may be odd because of their objects. But there seems to be no argument from the fact that people desire some very odd things to the conclusion that ordinary moral categories cannot be applied to them. An assumption of bland uniformity is not a prerequisite of a moral community. Nonetheless one may feel there is a limit. We would withhold full commendation from someone who experienced strong depraved desires even if he heroically resisted them. It is better to be a non-practising necrophile than a practising one. But the difficulty of accepting such a person should not be minimised.

It used to be fashionable to complain about being treated as an object. This was thought to be not merely unpleasant, but destructive of personal status. We are, however, objects for each other in all sorts of ways. It is this fact that raises problems for personal knowledge and interpersonal relations. Even at the level of perception, problems arise from the mere fact that we can see and be seen. The peeping Tom looks at people in ways incompatible with respecting them as persons. But it would be an extreme reaction to the peeping Tom to wish that one were invisible; and an even more extreme reaction to believe that one, or at least one's true self, *is* invisible. The rhetoric of treating people as subjects, not as objects, may be overdone: nevertheless an important point remains. Being the object of certain desires is not only unpleasant, but unlivable with. Some desires are destructive of the status of the object of desire.

We are talking of extreme cases, but not just fantastical examples. In the case of sexual harassment, one is fancied inopportunely; but the necrophile fancies one dead. We can recognise the fact, but we cannot live with the relationship. At the very least the necrophile is required not just to control his desires but to take steps to rid himself of them. There is no acceptable manifestation of necrophiliac desire, not even self-control.

It is not simply that necrophilia is a vice, and consequently there is no virtuous expression of it. There is no viable community between the necrophile and the object of his desire, and consequently normal attitudes to desire collapse, including the ways in which they are normally assessed, approved and disapproved, excused or condemned. The relationship between adversaries at war is an extreme one, but it has been regulated in numerous ways so that, even as they strive to bring about each others' deaths, there can be sympathy and pity, tolerance and admiration. There is no such common ground between the psychopathic killer and his victim.

Anthony Kenny remarks:

> ...the only attitude which [society] can adopt towards the class of criminals is to aim to eliminate it.
>
> (Kenny, 1978, p. 76)

This seems an exaggeration. It may be true in some abstract sense. But in any real state positive steps to accommodate criminals are taken and have to be taken. It is not just the cynical observation that some criminals, in some societies, provide a service, like black marketeers or brothel keepers. All communities must be able to accept a certain amount of rule-breaking. War, again, provides an analogy. All societies must, in some abstract sense, aim to eliminate enemy soldiers, but they must also find ways to accept the fact that in war, which they are unlikely to avoid forever, there will be enemy soldiers and killing them is only one of a number of possible ways of coming to terms with them. Not all crimes threaten the structure of society. Not all wars are wars of survival. Similarly most desires can be accommodated, even when they are unwelcome. But there are desires which are so destructive of personal relations that there is no available response to them. Even condemnation seems comically inappropriate.

The spontaneous reaction which takes the grossly depraved desires of the psychopath as sufficient evidence of insanity depends on the thought that there is something deeply unintelligible about such desires. But what? We have no difficulty in understanding what the child murderer wants, or what desires the sadistic killer is satisfying. It is rather that we cannot gain insight into the psychopathic mentality by imagining ourselves acting on such desires or being the objects of them. We can, of course, imagine ourselves as victims, but this is a nightmare, not an exercise in empathetic understanding. This inability is not a failure of imagination, but an indication that there is nothing there to imagine. It is not that x is a sensible object of desire whereas y is not. It is rather that a life in which y is an object of desire is one we cannot share, imagine or relate to.

irresistible desires

Another way in which the issue of responsibility may arise is if the object of desire is so bizarre that we are inclined to believe that the desire must be unusual in other ways as well, and that the abnormality of the person is unlikely to be restricted to this one feature of life. The obvious move here is to talk about irresistible desires. Irresistibility is just the sort of oddity that would be relevant to responsibility because it is incompatible with voluntariness. We feel, if only we could decide whether a person's desires were irresistible or just very strong, we could decide the issue of responsibility. But this is to state the problem quite the wrong way round. The phrases 'irresistible desire' and 'irresistible impulse' are unhappy ways of saying that this desire is not the desire of a normally responsible person. Irresistibility is not the highest degree on the Richter scale of desires. It is not on the scale at all. Desires can be weak, moderate, very strong, as strong as you like. Weak or strong, whether they can be resisted depends on the person whose desires they are. We hide sweets from three-year-olds because we do not expect them to do anything other than demand sweets if they can see them. On occasion, they can be easily distracted, showing that their desire for sweets, far from being strong was in fact quite weak, though they, being three, do not resist it. The problem is not to assess the desire: is it resistible or not? but to assess the person: can they resist their desires or not?

Desires tend to get satisfied, which is one of the nice things about them – in this they are different from fantasies and wishful thinking. It is equally important to say that the desires of the normally responsible person need not get satified. Being minimally accountable for one's behaviour involves, among other things, having desires, some of which are trivial, some of which are important, some of which will come into conflict with other desires or with overall objectives. It is part of what we mean by attributing responsibility to someone that he manages his desires and is not just buffeted by them. In this respect moral competence is no different from any other competence. To say that someone can play squash is to say that there are certain things he can do pretty well, for example make contact with the ball. Someone who consistently missed the ball would not be said to be playing squash, but playing it very badly. The most we would say is that he was trying to hit the ball with a view to learning to play squash. One can do badly in an activity only if one has some competence in that activity.

It is an analogous argument that lies behind the suspicion that psychopathic desires raise problems about responsibility. Any minimally responsible person who experienced such desires would realise that not acting on them was an absolute priority. To say that someone is morally responsible is not to make a neutral statement about his psychological abilities; it is to ascribe to him at least a minimal degree of moral competence, i.e. he has to be pretty good.

morality and desire

A third way in which the desires of psychopath may seem irrational is when the moral strategies that refer to desires break down. There comes a stage in cases of gross depravity when we feel that any moral response is pointless. This indicates we have crossed a boundary, but the boundary is not between sanity and insanity, nor between the voluntary and the involuntary. It is between behaviour which is comprehensible and containable within moral relations and institutions, and behaviour which is not.

For example, desires are often referred to by way of excuse or mitigation. We put a crime down to weakness of will, rather than to malice. The weak-willed person satisfies his desires even when he knows he ought not to. He will say as much, he will show signs of remorse, of struggle, of temporary successes and frequent failures. Such a person – which is everyone of us, in some areas of our lives – is well within the moral sphere. It is just such a person who requires the encouragements and dissuasions, all the resources of our moral system. Yet there is a limit to how weak-willed a person can get and still count as morally responsible. Weakness of will is not a medical concept like poor eyesight. It is a moral assessment; it refers to a moral failure of a particular sort. Whether it is used as an excuse or a condemnation, it ascribes moral strengths as well as weaknesses.

Socrates argued that no-one knowingly performs an action they believe to be wrong. He denied the possibility of weakness of will. This claim seems to contradict our most familiar moral experience. Yet the paradox may not be so paradoxical here. Not any behaviour can be explained by saying: he knew enough to act well, but he gave in to strong desire, i.e. he was in all other respects a normally responsible person, only he gave in to strong desire on this occasion. The criteria of a weak will are absent or present only in a minimal or inappropriate way. In extreme cases, the grossness of the capitulation excludes weakness of will as an account of the behaviour. Contemplating such actions and the desires which those actions satisfied we might say: 'no-one can be as weak-willed as *that*'.

Babuta and Bragard make the suggestion that Dennis Nilsen, who killed fifteen young men in London between 1978 and 1983, might have been found guilty of manslaughter, not murder, on the grounds that he was guilty of recklessness and negligence. This suggestion is motivated by a determination to fit Nilsen into the categories we would apply to standard cases of wrongdoing. They explicitly rely on an analogy with reckless driving. But it seems inappropriate and wide of the mark. Losing one parent is a misfortune, but, Oscar Wilde's Aunt Augusta thought, losing two looks like carelessness. What would she have said about Nilsen with his fifteen murders and eight attempts? One cannot kill fifteen people recklessly or negligently, not at any rate in the circumstances in which Nilsen found himself. The authors know this. It is not the killings that were reckless or negligent:

> ...it is possible to see how he might also have been found guilty of recklessness and negligence. Recklessness for knowingly getting drunk in order to be able to carry out the murders; negligence for never stopping to work out the implications and significance of his developing neuroses.
>
> (Babuta and Bragard, 1988, p. 95)

Apart from the legal point that getting drunk *in order to be able to* commit a crime would not constitute any sort of defence, these remarks lead us away from where we want to be, though they do suggest an interesting new crime, drunk in charge of a neurosis. We want to address the problem of what to say about a person who intentionally kills a number of people, because he wants to, and who is, we suspect, seriously mentally abnormal. It does not help to find him guilty of some other offence located back in the process by which he arrived at the state in which his crimes became possible.

Lying at the back of the opinions expressed by Babuta and Bragard is a rejection of the view that the psychopathic killer is an alien, with a psychology that bears little or no resemblance to the normal, to our own. They cite the psychologist Anthony Storr and the philosopher, Mary Midgley, to establish that:

> the individual who rapes and murders a child is not quite so
> remote from ordinary people as we would like to believe.
>
> (Babuta and Bragard, 1988, p. 59)

How close different abnormalities are to the broad band of behaviour which passes as normal is an empirical matter, but even in the cases of severe abnormalities, the differences must not be represented as undermining 'the unity of all human motivation' (Midgley, 1984, p. 20). What goes into the psychological make-up of the aberrant person are the same ingredients that constitute the normal. A different cocktail maybe, but the same human ingredients, anger, desire, resentment, contempt.

Nevertheless, this commitment to the continuity of human behaviour and the parallel rejection of fantastical accounts of the origin of evil do not compel us to apply the same moral categories to all members of the human species. The suggestion is not that the psychopath has an alien psychology but that we cannot understand acts of extreme depravity in the terms of everyday moral exchanges, and this is one of the phenomena behind the claim that psychopathic behaviour is irrational.

The psychopath presents a problem because it is unclear how his undoubted abnormality of mind affects his responsibility. It would seem that there must be some relevant cognitive or volitional disability. Unlike the legally insane, however, the psychopath is not so cognitively disturbed as to be unaware of the true nature of his actions. Therefore the failure must be a failure of control. For this reason, attention shifts to emotions, moods, desires and other aspects of affective experience. If there is anything about the psychopathic personality which threatens responsibility, then, it is normally thought, the psychopath must either have desires the rest of us do not experience, or his desires must be unusually, perhaps irresistibly, strong. The three considerations concerning psychopathic desire we have just presented do not rely on either of these ideas. They all terminated, however, in conclusions that have an important similarity. They call in question, from different points of view, the *autonomy* of the psychopath. The implication is that interpreting the problem posed by the psychopath in terms of passivity, whether it be irresistible impulses or overwhelmingly strong desires, is to misconstrue what is in reality an autonomy problem.

The first suggestion was that we cannot relate to a life dominated by the sort of violent desires which characterise the psychopath. The second was that the psychopath does not resist the desires that a normally responsible person would resist. Finally, it was argued that attempts to apply normal moral strategies to the affective life of the grossly depraved are clearly fatuous.

It is as if psychopath does not inhabit his own personality and act happily within it. All of us experience, from time to time, aspects of our own characters as alien, and consequently restrictive, or our own desires as external forces that threaten our well-being. It may be something as simple as smoking, which one day is the source of much pleasure and contentment, and the next a form of self-inflicted servitude. One's image of oneself changes from the debonair smoker in his quilted smoking jacket to the craven addict rummaging through other people's ashtrays. It is not that overnight the causal relationship between the person and the smoking habit is transformed from one which encourages, or at least allows for, personal freedom to one that inhibits or destroys it. Rather it is that the changed perception of smoking makes the habit unavailable as an expression of autonomous action. And yet one smokes.

The argument is not that there is no more compulsion or automatism in psychopathic behaviour than in normal. There may well be. If there is, there will be empirical evidence to that effect, and we may expect psychiatrists to be in possession of that evidence and to be in the best position to assess it. The argument is that there need not be such compulsion in order for us to find grounds for withholding responsibility. It would be sufficient if the psychopath relates to his own personality in a way which is different from normal, and which prevents him from endorsing his own actions. What we would have to accept is not that the psychopath lacks control in relation to his own personality, desires and emotions, but that he lacks autonomy.

The whole import of this section is contained in one remark of Dennis Nilsen:

> I cannot judge or see myself in any of it.
>
> (Masters, 1986 p. 135)

One's image of oneself changes from the debonair smoker to the craven addict.

notes

The following are the principal philosophers on whom we have relied in considering the relationship between people's characters and their responsibility for their actions:

Aristotle (384-322 BC), in his *Ethics*, considers what traits of character ought to be cultivated so that people can realise their potential, live a good life and attain happiness.

Descartes (1596-1650) was a philosopher, mathematician and scientist. The radical dualism between body and soul which he formulated is nowadays more or less universally rejected. Yet it tends to emerge, unofficially, in issues of responsibility, as in other areas, where there is a need to talk about the inner, subjective experience of individuals.

John Stuart Mill (1806-73) was the outstanding spokesman for Utilitarianism and Libertarianism, and a strong advocate of women's suffrage. His essay 'On Liberty' deals with issues of political freedom concerning the relationship between the individual citizen and the state. In elaborating his political views he produces a picture of the mature, responsible individual who is capable of exercising personal freedom.

Jean-Paul Sartre (1905-80) was a novelist and playwright as well as the most celebrated of the existentialist philosophers. A member of the French Resistance during the Second World War, he insisted on people's radical freedom and responsibility in the face of the collapse of social structures. The slogan 'man's existence precedes his essence' sums up his view that human nature is chosen and self-determined, not an inherited structure which determines behaviour and limits our possibilities.

Books and articles referred to in this chapter:
Aristotle, 1984, *Ethics*, trans. J.A.K. Thomson (Harmondsworth, Penguin Books).
Babuta, Subniv and Bragard, Jean-Claude, 1988, *Evil* (London, George Weidenfeld and Nicolson).
Descartes, 1975, *Discourse on Method and the Meditations* (Harmondsworth, Penguin Books).
Kenny, A., 1978, *Freewill and Responsibility* (London, Boston, Routledge and Kegan Paul).
Masters, Brian, 1986, *Killing for Company* (London, Cornet).
Midgley, Mary, 1984, *Wickedness* (London, Routledge and Kegan Paul).
Mill, J.S., 1968, *Utilitarianism, On Liberty, and Considerations on Representative Government* (London, Dent).
Sartre, J.-P., 1980, *Existentialism and Humanism* (London, Methuen).
Sartre, J.-P., 1981, *Sketch for a Theory of the Emotions* (London, Methuen).
Williams, B., 1985, *Ethics and the Limits of Philosophy* (London, Fontana).
Wootton, B., 1959, *Social Science and Social Pathology* (London, George Allen & Unwin).

5: autonomy

moral perspectives on mental abnormality
The law on diminished responsibility follows a commonsense
route. The defence is based on serious abnormality of mind,
which justifies a verdict different from the one which would be
delivered on a normal offender. The reason why serious abnormality effects the reduction in verdict is that it affects the
responsibility of the offender. And without the abnormality
there would be no reason to reduce the level of responsibility.
Both elements are necessary.

There is a class of offenders who present the special problem
that although they are indisputably abnormal, their abnormality
removes neither their ability to know what they are doing nor
their capacity to form the intention necessary for the crime to
be imputed to them. For this reason, attention has shifted from
cognitive to affective capacities, i.e. from questions of understanding to questions of feeling and desire. This shift, which
seems natural and inevitable, can be detected in the history of
the criticism of legal insanity which in England resulted in the
introduction of the plea of diminished responsibility.

The next question that arises is: on what grounds do the
desires and feelings of the seriously abnormal excuse? The
conclusion of the last chapter was that in so far as we remain
at the level of psychological states and capacities we fall short
of issues of responsibility. It is only in the light of the *moral*
implications of serious abnormal personalities that conclusions
concerning diminished responsibility can be drawn. It is necessary to be as explicit as possible on this point, because it is

contentious and it complicates the issues.

Why is it not possible to conclude from the psychological diagnosis to lack of responsibility, directly, without the introduction of any moral issues? Why is it only when the psychological peculiarities are viewed in a moral light that they produce the relevant consideration? If lack of responsibility could be established simply on the basis (such as it is) of psychological diagnosis, the issue would be factual; it would avoid contestable value claims. Why are psychiatric and legal considerations not sufficient to decide the issue of responsibility?

One answer would be that psychiatry is not yet in a position to provide incontestable testimony sufficient to determine the issue. Unfortunately it is unlikely that there will ever come a time when the matter will be scientifically determinable. The difficulty lies in the irreducible differences between law, morality and medical science. As Doctor Bowden said in the Nilsen trial, '...diminished responsibility is not an illness like the 'flu but a subsection of the Homicide Act' (Masters, 1986, pp. 233-4). There is, therefore, no hope that medical science will ever settle the issues of responsibility. Diminished responsibility is a legal not a medical matter. Furthermore 'mental responsibility' on which the legal decision concerning diminished responsibility is supposed to be based is neither a medical nor a legal, but a personal, moral matter. The result is that, at least theoretically, psychiatrists are two steps back from the final issue of legal liability. Between their diagnosis and the verdict two judgements intervene: one concerns the relation between mental abnormality and 'mental responsibility'; the other, the relation between the degree of impairment of responsibility and liability to the verdict of murder or manslaughter.

There is no more reason to think that psychiatrist ought to decide the fate of deviant offenders than to think that doctors ought to referee boxing bouts. The comparison is not as fanciful as it may appear at first. Boxers are required to pass a regular medical examination which determines whether they are fit to fight. Fitness to fight is, in the terminology of Hart's paper, 'The Ascription of Responsibilities and Rights', a 'defeasible' concept. It is not that 'fitness to fight' is a medical category, but

Fighting is not a matter for doctors.

rather that everyone (of the right sex, age, nationality, etc.) is fit to fight unless they suffer from one or more of a number of disabilities, injuries, or diseases. Whether or not such conditions are present is a medical matter. Doctors may also intervene during a fight to determine whether an injury is serious enough to require that the fight be stopped.

However, there is another way in which a man's fitness to fight arises in boxing other than through the intervention of doctors. A referee may decide that a contestant is unfit to continue. The difference between the referee and the doctor is that the referee makes his decision as a fight official, within the fight situation. Normally when he makes such a decision he does so on the same sort of grounds that a doctor would take into account when making a diagnosis. But the referee's decision is not an amateur diagnosis. His criteria have to do directly with boxing performance, though they may encompass the same considerations that the doctor takes into account.

In so far as the doctor restricts himself to medical matters his findings do not touch the issue of fitness to fight. That is why it is grotesque to suggest that doctors should regard it as part of their medical duties to referee boxing contests. Fighting is not a matter for doctors. Doctors are two steps back from the decision concerning fitness to fight. Given the medical diagnosis the question remains: ought a person in this state to be considered fit to fight? Which diagnosable, physical conditions constitute fitness to fight is not a medical decision. The referee, on the other hand, as an official of the Boxing Authority, is concerned precisely with fighting.

The second question which comes between any diagnosis and the decision is a matter of principle. Some radical critics of the noble art of self-defence will argue that no-one is fit to fight. They are not disputing the medical diagnosis; they are expressing their opinion that fighting is not fit for people however healthy. Someone who has a principled objection to boxing is not impressed by a medical certificate which says this person is fit to fight. They are right to remain unmoved because fitness to fight is not a medical issue. The doctor's judgements determine the issue of fitness to fight only if these two questions have been resolved, while the referee's decision is taken in a situation where these issues are regarded as already settled.

The jury are to be compared with the referee. They are not there as amateur psychiatrists, even though they will take into account the same matters that concern the psychiatrists. The psychological states and capacities that psychiatrists report on provide grounds for decisions about responsibility only when they are subsumed into the moral domain. Interpreting psychiatric diagnoses within the context of moral relationships is the role of the jury.

In the last chapter we commented on the unsatisfactory

phrase in section 2 of the Homicide Act, 'such abnormality of mind...as substantially impaired his responsibility for his acts ...'. We can now understand why the terminology is inadequate. The inference from mental abnormality to mental responsibility involves a move from psychiatric diagnosis to moral assessment. There is nothing wrong with the inference; it is not an instance of the fallacy of infering a value statement from a factual statement, because it makes use of moral assumptions and beliefs. What is unsatisfactory is that it is represented in the Act as if it was a causal connection, when what is in fact involved is bringing the mental abnormality of the offender into the ambit of moral response to see what attitudes and reactions to the offender are possible.

One indication of the move from psychiatric report to moral assessment is the shift from talking in terms of control to talking in terms of authority. Whether the seriously abnormal offender can control his impulses is not only a difficult question to answer, it is not the right question. It is always possible to ask: why should we hold people responsible for their actions on the grounds that they can control themselves? There is not a corresponding question in relation to authority. Someone who acts authoritatively is accountable. For this reason we concentrate not on the issue of voluntariness but on the issue of autonomy. It is in terms of autonomy that philosophers have attempted to capture the issues of authority at which we have now arrived.

autonomy
Autonomy means self-government. It was originally and remains still, in its central sense, a political notion. It was first elaborated in the context of the struggle of the Greek city states for independence from the Persian Empire. It applies to states and corporate bodies. It sounds natural to say, for example, that the BMA is an autonomous institution; whereas the claim that a person is autonomous still has an academic ring to it, despite the weight that the notion has borne in moral theory.

The application of autonomy to individuals rather than corporate bodies, to the personal and moral domain, rather than to the political, is analogical. Like all analogies it may be misleading; and, like all analogies, it will, sooner or later, limp. It may well be that the independence of states in an ultimately lawless international context is not a good model for personal independence. Even if this fundamental doubt is allayed, there are problems about how much of the original analogue is to be carried over – what features and conditions of corporate bodies are we seriously applying to individuals, and which are to be quietly forgotten in the projection of the comparision. Inevitably the term is used to mean different things. Sometimes it implies little more than doing what one wants. Sometimes it has been used to express an aggressive liberalism – doing one's own thing. A more ambitious sense relates the word not to actions but to the whole of life; in this sense it means choosing one's own objectives, having a life plan over which one has considerable control. Kant made the idea central to his explanation of morality and freedom. He explains it in terms of self-legislation, of living according to laws that one imposes on one's self.

The ambiguity of the idea of personal autonomy causes real difficulties. Yet the concept has proved irresistible to moral philosophers. If we talk about people in terms of their autonomy, we make it clear from the start that we are concerned not just with what they do or can do, but with the authority with which they do what they do. We focus not on their physical and psychological abilities, but on the legitimacy of their actions. In a word, autonomy is an authority, not a power concept.

In the *Gorgias*, Socrates ridicules Polus when he confuses authority and power. On this view, he claims, a dagger is a great instrument of government, and the armed assassin a great statesman. The wicked thought that Polus is right and Socrates piously wrong overlooks the fact that cynicism about political power presupposes at least the idea of the possibility of legitimacy. If we are to talk about people in terms of autonomy it is essential that we preserve this line of thought.

It is the moral kernel of Kant's position: just as an autonomous state has authority, not just *de facto* control over its citizens, so autonomous individuals have authority over their actions. We should take a minute out to be surprised at this idea. It is, after all, not a natural way of speaking. People are said to have authority over other people, or over an institution, or in a place, or at a time, but not over their own actions. Do we not just act? We may, in some circumstances, be said to have, or not to have, control over our actions. But when are we said to have authority over them?

Similar doubts have been raised in relation to the concept of responsibility. Do we ever claim responsibility for actions? People are responsible for ensuring a task is carried out, for fulfilling their duty, for the behaviour of others who have a special relationship to them, for some of the consequences of their actions, but not, it may seem, for their actions themselves.

The parallel problem that now arises as regards autonomy is this: how could it make sense to talk of one's authority in relation to one's own actions? We would only talk this way if we were striving to say something special. The special thought is that the autonomous person not only acts, not only controls what he does, he stamps his authority on what he does; he gives his actions, at least sometimes, a particular legitimacy.

a Platonic example

A dramatic illustration of autonomy understood in this sense is to be found in the Platonic dialogue, the *Crito*. There Socrates defends his decision to submit to execution, even though he was unjustly condemned, and though escape into exile was easy and expected. He imagines the laws of Athens, personified, talking to him. They have plenty to say, but the culmination of their argument is this:

> Do you intend, then, to avoid well governed states and the higher forms of human society? and if you do, will life be worth living? Or will you approach these people and have the impudence to converse with them? What arguments will you use, Socrates? The same which you used here, that goodness and integrity, institutions and laws, are the most precious possessions of mankind? Do you not think that Socrates and everything about him will appear in a disreputable light? You certainly ought to think so. But perhaps you will retire from this

part of the world and go to Crito's friends in Thessaly? That is the home of indiscipline and laxity, and no doubt they will enjoy hearing the amusing story of how you managed to run away from prison by arraying yourself in some costume or putting on a shepherd's smock or some other conventional runaway's disguise, and altering your personal appearance...and where will your discussions about goodness and uprightness be then, we should like to know?

(Plato, 1978, pp. 94-5)

The central point is that outside of Athens, outside of its constitution and laws, Socrates would lose his voice. He could, of course, still speak and with his usual wit and intelligence. But everything he had said and done, had been said and done as a citizen, albeit an incurably dissident citizen of Athens. Outside of the city nothing of that would be left. His actions would lose any value he thought them to have. He would be forced to play a part. This is the point of the allusion to the shepherd's smock. He would have to dress up, like an actor. He would lose the ability to speak for himself in his own voice.

These changes would come about without any psychological alteration in Socrates himself. They flow from the change of status and the altered social relationships consequent on the shift from citizen to fugitive. In an obvious sense he would be more free at dinner parties in Thessaly than on death row in Athens. What he would lose is his autonomy.

the need for common values
The behaviour of Socrates is a dramatic example of autonomy. But it is also contentious and difficult for us to accept. The reason for our difficulty is that we do not tie our sense of our own autonomy so tightly into our citizenship. We do appreciate the disadvantages and indeed the tragedy of being stateless. But we are inclined to believe in, or at least hope for, a degree of personal autonomy which would be unaffected by our political acceptability in this or that state. This cosmopolitanism may be an illusion. Perhaps I can be autonomous in London New York or Zurich, but what about Tehran? Illusion or not, the fundamental Socratic position is unaffected. Autonomy is possible only in contexts where questions of authority arise.

There can be authority only in social contexts where issues of right and wrong, claim and counter-claim are relevant. To have such situations two things are required. First, there must a public domain structured by standards, ideals, expectations, conventions and rules. Secondly, the individual must operate within that domain. For Socrates the domain was Athenian citizenship.

The commitment of Socrates to his city was extreme. The trouble with extreme examples is that though they may capture the imagination for two thousand years, they can boggle the mind just as persistently. So, it may be better to leave Socrates being wonderful in his cell, and take less intimidating examples.

Making a move in chess, signing a cheque or giving someone permission to drive your car are all small exercises in autonomy. It is one thing to follow a game of chess played by someone else, and another to make a move for yourself. It is one thing to spend money – I can even spend your money – but I alone can sign my own cheques. I can incite someone to drive off in your car; I can give permission only in the case of my own.

Compare these simple cases to eating. The cow untethered is, in one perfectly good sense, free. It chomps where it will. Libertarians may insist that the free range cow is free only in an attenuated sense, which does not bear on issues of responsibility. In order to have a free, as opposed to an unconstrained agent, they may insist on a condition that a cow could not meet. It must be true of a genuinely free agent, that it could have done other than it did. But why should that feature, of itself, produce the freedom that determines responsibility? Why should flexibility of choice and behaviour decide the issue of responsibility? It may be a necessary condition of holding someone responsible that their actions be voluntary and undetermined, but it is not a sufficient condition. That someone acted voluntarily, or that they could have done other than they did, does not mean that they acted autonomously.

There may have been a time when human eating was indistinguishable from the bovine. But now it is enmeshed in a complex net of social expectations: how much to eat, how to eat, in what order, when and where. Given all this, it becomes possible to eat well or badly, to be or not to be an autonomous eater, and consequently to be responsible for what one eats and how one eats. In Stoppard's play *Professional Foul,* the dire Professor Stone makes the point that in the right context, for example an eating competition, it is possible for Mary to say to John, 'Well, you didn't eat very well, but at least you ate well'. Stoppard may have been aware that the remarks of Professor Stone, which represent philosophy at its most degenerate, depend ultimately on the same issues of individual rights and the rules of the community that Professor Anderson raises in his speech at the end of the play. Whether the irony of the playwright was intended to extend to this point or not, the position can be stated in the comic, crass terms of eating or in the solemn rhetoric of political philosophy: there is no individual autonomy outside of a system of communal values.

The examples introduced above, playing chess, having a bank account and borrowing and lending property, all allow for autonomous action because they involve acting legitimately, in one's own name. No degree of voluntariness, spontaneity of action, or flexibility of behaviour could amount to authoritative action.

The point is a familiar one. The distinction between liberty and licence depends upon it. If the distinction is to be saved from collapse into useless subjectivism, according to which one man's liberty is another man's licence, it must incorporate common standards. It is, of course, essential to any substantial liberalism that one respects the freedom of others, even when one disagrees with them or disapproves of what they are doing. But if one can find nothing to admire in their behaviour, if one cannot even place their actions in the context of shared standards and values, then their exercise of liberty can seem nothing other than the throwing about of weight. Milton was right to place a morality requirement on freedom, if freedom is to be thought of as desirable in itself:

> License they mean when they cry, Liberty!
> For who loves that, must first be wise and good.
>
> (Milton, 1971, p. 78)

Suppose one plays beach cricket with the children, and one of them grabs the bat and says 'I'll bat first'. Well, that is one thing, and we don't much approve of it. We usually respond by offering them a rule, 'Let's bat in order of age, starting with the youngest'. If during the game the child insists 'It's my turn now', that is not a lawless assertion of wilfulness. It involves a recognition of turns, yours and mine, as well as his. It is also, of course, a personal claim, a demand for recognition. What distinguishes the wilfulness of the first demand from the autonomy of the second is the acceptance of a common system of values and rules.

the engagement of the individual
There can be no autonomy without a social context in which the individual can act. Equally the individual must be incorporated into the system. You must apply for a bank account, if you want to sign your own cheques. You must join the game, if you want to take your turn. It is an important feature of the moral world that one does not have to apply, indeed one cannot apply for membership. This points up a fundamental difference between morality and other more restricted social contexts with which it may be compared. Whether one is a moral agent does not depend on choice. But the fact that the moral dimension is inalienable does not depend on the individual having in himself all that is required for a moral life. It does not imply that autonomy, and consequently responsibility, are not as dependent on the social world in the moral case, as they are in the legal or financial spheres. One cannot opt into or out of the moral world, but that does not weaken the dependence of the individual on the community.

If a person is to be autonomous and to be held responsible, her presence must be acknowledged. This does not mean that she has to be accepted by this or that individual on any particular occasion; but neither does it mean merely the possibility of her being accepted. It means that authoritative presence involves acknowledgement. There is no membership without acceptance. Acceptance is not the recognition of membership; it enters into the constitution of membership.

Without mutual acknowledgement there is no cohabitable world of morality or law, beach cricket or bank accounts.

Acknowledgement is not a form of knowledge. To acknowledge someone is not in itself to know any facts about them, not even psychological facts about them. Just as to greet someone in the street, which is a form of acknowledgement, is not a sort of knowledge. Consequently, the claim that autonomy involves acknowledgement, is not to say that someone is autonomous if someone else knows they are, or says they are. One is not a member in virtue of the fact that anyone knows one is a member – even if that anyone is the membership secretary. One is a member because one is accepted. Once one is accepted, others can know or not know it. Even the membership secretary may forget or lose his records. Acknowledgement then is a form of acceptance, not of knowledge.

Suppose there was a society in which chess had an awesome status – say it had some dread religious significance. The laws of genetics and child psychology would not thereby be changed. Every now and then the population would throw up a Bobby Fischer, who, at the age of six, we would say, could play better chess than all but a handful of adults. But the people of the chess-ridden society need not believe this at all. They may regard it as obvious that their little Bobbies cannot even make a move, chess being far too momentous a business for the involvement of children. They may think this, knowing everything we know about the psychological capacities of children. They may regard the prodigies as possessed, as oracles to be hidden away. The more secular among them may give the children the status of books or computers to be consulted and used, but which cannot make a move for themselves. Perhaps it is more likely, human nature being what it is, that the citizens of the chess-ridden society would simply fail to notice the capacities of the children, or would find some way to discount them. Children who showed an unhealthy, precocious interest in chess, would be locked in cellars, or given sedatives, or have their arms strapped to their sides, so that they could not play with their little pieces.

If the example seems silly, ask: isn't this just what has been done to many groups – children, women, barbarians – in many cultures, including our own? However, the point is not that the incapacities, which we think we detect in others, may be restrictions that we impose upon them. Rather, whatever people's psychological and intellectual capacities may be, their ability to act *authoritatively* is always a function of what is acceptable and where the restrictive lines are to be drawn.

'ascriptivism'

It is important at this point to prevent a misunderstanding. Responsibility is a social concept that refers to the relationship of accountability that holds between persons within a community. Autonomy is the individual side of the responsibility penny. As we have just said, autonomy also can be understood only in a social context; it is a function of acknowledgement and acceptability. In this sense, both concepts are conventional. They are logically dependent on human institutions and rules of conduct.

None of this implies that a person is responsible or autonomous because somebody thinks they are, or says they are, or in any other way ascribes these states to them. The claim is that responsibility and autonomy are constituted by certain social interactions and reactions. Questions about responsibility are, consequently, questions about the sorts of relationship we have or could have. Such relationships are not called into being by someone's say so. Nor are they dissolved by someone's refusal to admit their existence. They are not generated by *speech acts*. The notion of a speech act is that sometimes, simply by an appropriate utterance, an act is performed and certain consequences follow. A person's name is determined simply by what the right people (usually the parents) call them on the right occasion (e.g. in the office of the Registrar of Births). The accused becomes the convicted when the jury delivers its verdict. H.L.A. Hart caused a controversy when he applied this line of thought to action statements. He said that sentences such as 'he did it' which have traditionally been regarded as primarily descriptive sentences are, in their primary function, ascriptive. They are not factual statements that are true or false, but attributions of responsibility that express the taking up of an attitude towards the agent. This is implausible as regards action statements as a whole, and Hart later withdrew his thesis. Nevertheless it may continue to seem an attractive account of responsibility.

Concepts of responsibility standardly occur in situations in which we are attributing or withholding responsibility from others or claiming or disclaiming it for ourselves. There may be few occasions on which we report as a fact that so-and-so is responsible for his actions. Even so, this does not establish that responsibility is constituted by the ascription of responsibility. It does not mean that an individual is responsible because others ascribe responsibility to him, in the sense that he has his name because others have given it to him.

Peter Geach lampoons the suggestion that ascriptivism casts light on the foundations of responsibility by unearthing the word 'macarizing' which means 'calling someone happy':

> To call a man happy is not to characterize or describe his condition; macarizing a man is a special non-descriptive use of language. If we consider such typical examples of macarism as the Beatitudes, or again such proverbial expressions as 'happy the bride the sun shines on; happy are the dead that the rain rains on', we can surely see that these sentences are not used to convey propositions. How disconcerting and inappropriate was the reply, 'Yes, that's true' that a friend of mine got when he cited 'happy are the dead that the rain rains on' at a funeral on a rainy day! The great error of Utilitarianism was to suppose...

(Geach, 1960, p. 222)

This disdainful argument points up the trivialising effect of attempting to side-step substantial questions about responsibility by appealing to uses of language. Holding someone responsible and being held responsible oneself are not actions, like christening the baby. If they are not actions, they are not speech acts. Nor are they practices, like human sacrifice. If they are not practices, they are not linguistic practices. They are aspects of an interpersonal relationship.

The point of insisting that autonomy involves the acknowledgement of others is to emphasise its dependence on social realities, not to claim that it is brought into being by the legislative act of any individual or institution.

partial autonomy

We have explained responsibility in terms of autonomy. It is, therefore, natural to look for an explanation of diminished responsibility in terms of partial autonomy. Both notions present difficulties. J.L. Mackie, for example, says that diminished responsibility is nonsensical, because it involves the idea that someone half did what they did, that they both did and didn't do it.

> It must be admitted that the notion of a lower degree of responsibility is a confused one: it suggests that the action in question is a completely wrong one, but that the agent didn't quite commit it, doesn't fully own it...What must be meant is that there is full responsibility but for a less wrong act...Where there is said to be reduced responsibility, the act in question...is of a sort less strongly disapproved than others. It is the emotion of disapproval which admits of degrees.
>
> (Mackie, 1985, p. 41)

This passage does us the service of briefly and clearly contradicting two of the main themes of this book. Mackie believes that being less responsible can only mean being responsible for less. He does not believe it is possible to be more or less responsible for the same action. The source of this view is the idea that the only way responsibility for an action could be reduced is by attributing to the agent an intention to commit a less heinous offence. If the agent's intention is different, the action attributable to him is different. Consequently any diminution of responsibility can only mean that one is equally responsible for a different and lesser crime.

Secondly, disapproval is, according to Mackie, the only variable that could account for varying degrees of responsibility. If someone is held to be less than normally responsible, it must be that their actions are less than normally disapproved of. But this is clearly not the case. There is no tendency to disapprove less of a criminal act, because the perpetrator is abnormal, even to the point of legal insanity. Perhaps it is the agent, and not his act, that attracts less disapproval, whenever responsibility is withheld or reduced. This need not be the case, as I shall argue in the final chapter. Even if it is the case, the question remains: why do we disapprove less of the less responsible? We have already excluded, as the law demands, the possibility of an answer in terms of a less serious criminal intention. The only option is to return to the concept of responsibility itself. This is not an option for Mackie because, in his opinion, to attribute responsibility to an agent in relation to his act is to say that he caused it; to attribute diminished responsibility is to say he half-caused it, and this is incoherent.

But autonomy, and consequently responsibility, are not concepts of action, but concepts which relate to the authority with which actions are done. If one says, for example, of a child, that it is partially autonomous, one is not saying that it is autonomous in what it half did. One says that the child had some, though not full authority in doing what it did. If one says of a mentally ill person that their responsibility is diminished, one is saying that they cannot be treated as wholly answerable for what they do; their responsibility is limited in scope, in depth and in independence. Their responsibility is limited because their autonomy is limited. They are not allowed, and perhaps do not demand, full authority over their own actions.

Still there seems to be a problem. Someone can, legitimately, exercise more or less power; but how can they exercise power, more or less legitimately? If autonomy essentially involves acceptance, and if acceptance can in various ways be a matter of degree, then so can autonomy. Responsibility can be diminished or partial because there are degrees of autonomy; there can be degrees of autonomy because the extent to which we accept the authority of a person varies. Acceptance of authority, not disapproval is the variable on which diminished responsibility depends.

Consider teaching a small child to play Snap. One is aiming to get the child to take its turn, to make its claims and to submit its claims to objective assessment according to the rules. As Snap is one of the first card games that a child normally learns, one is trying to get the child to do these things, when it may have an insecure grip on the idea of turns and claims and rules. We use all sorts of little tactics. We delay our own calls. We make eyes when identical cards come up. We prompt. We make their calls for them. We let them win, because we also have to teach them what it is to win. As hour follows tedious hour, the child begins to act with more assurance and confidence. We gradually withdraw our support, until the child is truly playing its own hand for itself.

In this way we can see how there can be degrees of autonomy even in an activity as simple as Snap. It is not that the child half plays its cards. In taking its turns and making its claims, the child demands and is given greater and greater independence.

the autonomy of psychopathic offenders

The conclusion of Chapter 4 was that we cannot relate to a life dominated by the sort of violent desires which characterize the psychopath; minimal moral relations presume that those sorts of desires are not acted upon, are not even accepted into a person's life as conscious motives. Consequently, it was argued, attempts to apply normal moral strategies to the behaviour of the grossly depraved end in failure.

To hold people responsible for their actions is to react to them as autonomous agents. Reacting to them in this way means acknowledging their authority. Acknowledging their authority is only possible if we cohabit in an intelligible and worthwhile world. The psychopath presents us with a special problem: we do not know how to react to him and his crimes in a way that will produce an intelligible and worthwhile world. It is the failure of moral cohesion, not psychological incapacities, that makes it impossible for us to treat brutal psychopaths as fully responsible for their actions.

This breakdown in community between society and the offender is not always apparent nor is it ever complete. The enigmatic character of such people often allows for a surface normality and a sort of pretence in which behaviour associated with normal relationships is produced, but soullessly. They know their actions are disapproved of, but this knowledge remains unreal and external. Detachment and lack of remorse are among the most frequently noted of their characteristics. They realise they have broken the law, but seem not quite able to understand what all the fuss is about. (Perhaps a significant percentage of those who do understand what the fuss is about, never come to court. A third of those who commit homicide kill themselves before arrest (cf. Craft, 1984, p. 89). The majority of them have committed domestic crimes, the victims of which are spouses and children.) Robert Wilson observed of the child killer, Ian Brady:

> He reminded me, for all the world, of a man charged with nothing more serious than riding a bicycle without a rear light.
> (Wilson, 1987, p. 96)

Nilsen, who is not only intelligent and articulate, but in some ways sympathetic and sensitive, seems to lack a genuine appreciation of how other people think of him:

> It is an interesting comment on Nilsen's perception of reality that he could admit a series of ghastly acts, and be surprised if people reacted with hostility towards him.
> (Masters, 1986, p. 172)

Nilsen is not incapable of feeling guilt and remorse. The problem, which he recognises himself, is what weight is to be attached to any of his expressions of sorrow. The question is not: how can one tell whether he is telling the truth? The deeper question is: is he in a position to tell the truth? What stance can he adopt which would give him the right and the authority to express remorse?

> Words like 'sorry' hold little comfort for the bereaved. I mistrust my own inner sincerity to bear even to utter them.
> (Masters, 1986, p. 248)

decisions about responsibility

The decision about moral responsibility is itself a moral decision. It is made in the context of moral standards and codes of conduct on the basis of the person's character viewed from a moral perspective. A.I. Melden talking not about responsibility but about rights – another topic on which strongly opposed views are held – asks what evidence could there be which would establish that certain people have certain rights. What could it be in their behaviour or lives which would provide a foundation for the attribution of rights? His answer may seem discouraging:

> The philosophical understanding of the rights of human beings must come to rest on nothing less, and on nothing else than, this enormously complicated and moral form of life itself; in order to spell it out we would need to describe and comment on the most familiar of the endlessly varied and complicated ways in which in thoughts, actions, and feelings persons reveal themselves as the moral beings they are.
>
> (Melden, 1977, pp. 199-200)

We have faced the same question and given the same answer in relation to responsibility. The prospect of confronting juries with 'enormously complicated' and 'endlessly varied' considerations on which to base their verdict hardly recommends itself to lawyers or legislators. However, the endless complexity only arises when we attempt to spell it out for the purposes of philosophical understanding. The complexity of the basis on which the decision is made need not and better not be made explicit in the jury room. It is present in the richness of the moral life that the jury allegedly shares.

Responsibility concerns social relationships not inner states. Consequently the jury's task is not to guess from the outside what is already known from the inside, either by the accused himself, or, if he is sunk in illusion, at any rate by God. Nor will their verdict be correct only if it happily coincides with the deliverance of the conscience of the offender or the finding of an ideal court having all the psychological facts at its disposal.

The jury's task is difficult but it does not have that sort of impossibility about it. The decision concerns relationships, so the jury must relate as directly as possible to the accused. For this reason, the most important evidence before the court will be psychiatric reports which are based on interviews with the accused. In the circumstances these are likely to be the most reliable source of personal information. Even these, however, are incomplete without the direct participation of the accused.

On this point the philosophical account of responsibility is lent support by psychiatric and legal considerations.

Seymour Spencer, a forensic psychiatrist, makes the following comment about the requirements for an adequate presentation of the psychiatric evidence relevant to the issue of diminished responsibility:

> It is the author's experience that the full facts in an opposed Section 2 manslaughter case do not emerge until witnesses are examined and cross-examined, including the defendant when defence counsel has the courage (or temerity?) to call him. Depositions, proofs, social enquiry reports and examination of the defendant take the psychiatrist only so far down the road to understanding. Presence in court throughout the trial may add to it enormously, and also reduces the possibility of a strict judge ruling out elements of medical evidence as 'hearsay'.
>
> (Craft, 1984, p. 96)

Spencer is saying that, from a psychiatric point of view, satisfactory presentation of the relevant facts requires the fullest possible involvement of the defendant, including cross-examination. From a legal point of view also there is good reason to encourage the defendant to give evidence. In a plea of diminished responsibility the burden of proof is on the defence. It is difficult to see how a defendant can ask a jury to accept this plea if he refuses to make available the most valuable evidence. This is what he does if he declines to speak directly to the court. The presenting of psychiatric reports is a requirement, at least in practice, of the plea. No doubt there are overriding reasons for not making the testimony of the defendant a condition of the plea. Nonetheless the absence of direct testimony from the accused has to weaken the case that it is necessary for the defence to produce.

The above remarks are intended to explain how Section 2 of the Homicide Act or any other legislation which shares the same structure allows for a decision procedure concerning responsibility. They also give reason to believe that if the issue of responsibility is to come to trial at all, then this procedure, or one closely modelled on it, is necessary. However, it must be admitted that there are great difficulties in deciding issues of responsibility in courts. The formality of the court, the perilous situation of the defendant, the fact that all the major participants are likely to be strangers to each other prior to entering the court, all these factors and many others are obstacles in the path of the jury as it attempts to gain access to the personality of the defendant. It is on this access that the validity of the decision procedure depends.

Most of the suggestions that are currently put forward for the reform of the law are designed to remove the issue of responsibility from the courts and especially from juries. It would be better if reformers concentrated their efforts on introducing into law courts improved techniques for the eliciting and presentation of the relevant psychological evidence. Such techniques will not supplant adversarial questioning, but they could supplement it.

Courts have been persuaded to amend their procedures when dealing with, for example, children and the victims of rape. Why, for example, could the jury not see video tapes of, or even be present at interviews of, the defendant by psychiatrists? Such interviews could include types of questions which would normally be excluded by the laws of evidence, and more dynamic forms of inquiry than questioning which would not be permitted in court.

We can only presume to make decisions about people's responsibility if we can claim genuinely personal knowledge of them. In our individualistic culture we are sceptical about the possibility of acquiring personal knowledge of others even in favourable circumstances. The trappings of courts of law add special obstacles to those that already stand in the way of such knowledge. We should do whatever we can to remove them.

notes

Kant placed the concept of autonomy at the centre of his moral theory. It is because of his influence that autonomy plays an important part in many subsequent theories, which in other respects are far removed from the Kantian account of moral life. Kant's perplexing but beautiful ideas are expressed in: Kant, I., 1962, *Fundamental Principles of the Metaphysics of Ethics*, trans. Thomas K. Abbott (London, Longmans).

A short and readable introduction to the different accounts that have been given of the concept of autonomy and some of the problems that arise in relation to it, can be found in:

Lindley, R. 1986, *Autonomy* (Basingstoke, MacMillan).

The following articles were contributions to the dispute about 'ascriptivism', to which we have referred in this chapter:

Hart, H.L.A., 1948, 'The Ascription of Responsibilities and Rights', *Proceedings of the Aristotelian Society*, vol. XLIV.

P. Geach, 1960, 'Ascriptivism', *Philosophical Review*, vol. LXIX, pp. 221-25.

Pitcher, George, 1960, 'Hart on Action and Responsibility', *The Philosophical Review*, vol. LXIX, pp. 226-35.

Other works cited in this chapter:

Masters, Brian, 1986, *Killing for Company* (London, Cornet).

Milton, John, 'On the Detraction Which Followed Upon My Writing Certain Treatises', in 1971, *The English Poems of John Milton*, ed. H.C. Beeching (London, OUP).

Mackie, J.L., 1985, 'Responsibility and Language', in *Persons and Values*, pp. 28-45, (Oxford, Clarendon Press).

Melden, A.I., 1977, *Rights and Persons* (Berkeley and Los Angelos, University of California Press).

Plato, 1978, *Crito in The Last Days of Socrates*, trans. H. Tredennick, (Harmondsworth, Penguin Books), pp. 79-96.

Spencer Seymour, 1984, 'Homicide, Mental Abnormality and Offence', in Craft, Michael and Ann, *Mentally Abnormal Offenders* (London, Bailliere Tindall) pp. 106-13.

Stoppard, T., 1978, *Professional Foul* (London, Faber & Faber).

Wilson, R., 1987, *The Devil's Disciples* (London, Javelin Books).

6: personal knowledge

objections to responsibility

There are different reasons for being suspicious of the concept of responsibility. Consequently there are different motives that animate distrust of the practices, such as blaming, and institutions, such as law courts, which incorporate it. Broadly speaking the reasons fall into three categories. Firstly, responsibility may be thought to be incompatible with the world, scientifically understood. Secondly, some people suspect that the main function of the concept of responsibility is to licence such indefensible practices as retributive punishment, and to resist the reforming pressure to substitute diagnosis and therapy for vindictiveness and revenge. Finally, it is claimed that it is impossible to *know* whether anyone is responsible for their actions or not.

It is the first consideration, which raises the problems of determinism, that has preoccupied philosophers. The second and third types of objection, however, raise more practical concerns. We have attempted to meet the objections to responsibility which are based on moral grounds, by distinguishing the notion of responsibility from the notion of liability to punishment. If we maintain the distinction (which was one of the themes of Chapter 3), most of the moral objections to responsibility turn out to be objections to the theory and the practices of punishment. These criticisms can be accepted as enthusiastically as any penal reformer could wish, without weakening the idea of responsibility. It becomes possible to believe both that the more we hold people responsible for their actions the better, and that the less we punish the better.

The third category of objections remains to be considered and it concerns the issue which arose at the end of the last chapter. How can we know whether a person is responsible for their actions? This is a serious difficulty in view of the unusual and extreme personalities with which we are concerned. The serious difficulty will quickly change to downright impossibility if we bring to the problem false assumptions about personal knowledge in general.

Law courts must deal with all law-breakers, the brutal psychopath as well as the professional criminal and the petty thief. Few people object to that or find it a problem. But when the courts claim to determine matters that require intimate knowledge of the criminal, and deep assessments of his character, doubts may begin to emerge. These doubts go beyond the practical problems of whether the institutions of the court are specially well designed to acquire genuine knowledge of those who appear before it. They reach to the very possibility of acquiring such knowledge even in optimum conditions. Doubts which extend this far find contemporary thought in many respects a congenial environment. In our culture for which the paradigm of knowledge is empirical science, personal knowledge is an embarrassment, to which scepticism is a common reaction.

Is there something worth calling personal knowledge? Is our knowledge of persons a distinctive sort of knowledge, distinguishable from knowledge of the non-personal? Is what counts as personal knowledge (a) truly of *persons* and (b) is it truly *knowledge*?

Problems concerning knowledge of persons cannot be avoided in relation to responsibility. Responsibility is not an inner state. So the decision about responsibility does not require us to take an impossible peek into an essentially private world. However, that, in itself, is not the end of the problem. The alternative proposed, namely that responsibility is a social reality, does not mean that responsibility is an empirical concept that can be unproblematically applied to observable behaviour. Nor can the issue be side-stepped by claiming that responsibility is a status we confer, not a state we can become aware of, as if ascribing responsibility were like naming a ship.

Responsibility is a concept that can attach itself only to persons. If the concept of person is somehow or other dissolved into other concepts, for example into the concept of brain states or psychological states, then the concept of responsibility will disappear along with it. Or if we despair of attaining knowledge of persons and believe that we must be satisfied with knowledge of something other than persons, for example, patterns of behaviour, then we must lose confidence in our ascriptions of responsibility.

The requirement that personal knowledge be *truly of persons* is an attempt to say that we must not be satisified with something other than persons nor with some philosophical fantasy of what a person must be. It is not so easy to ensure that one's views are untainted by fantasies. In *A Chapter on Dreams* Robert Louis Stevenson expresses a straightforward view of persons. But he leads up to it with a reference to philosophical opinions which conflict with his own point of view. He is ruminating on the theme of literary inspiration and on the impression that his writings seem to emanate not from himself, but from 'some Brownie, some Familiar, some unseen collaborator, whom I keep locked in a back garret':

> For myself – what I call I, my conscious ego, the denizen of the pineal gland unless he has changed his residence since Descartes, the man with the conscience and the variable bank-account, the man with the hat and the boots, and the privilege of voting and not carrying his candidate at the general elections – I am sometimes tempted to suppose he is no story-teller at all, but a creature as matter of fact as any cheesemonger or any cheese, and a realist bemired up to the ears with actuality...
>
> (Stevenson, 1987, p. 207)

We must leave behind the theory that I call anything 'I', for 'I' is not a name. We must treat with suspicion the identification of myself with 'my conscious ego'. The pineal gland has long since been taken care of to most people's satisfaction. All the rest, however, is needed for a complete notion of person. We need individuals with their consciences, bank-accounts, boots, votes and their stories. Our thesis is that there is knowledge of persons in this complex but ordinary sense, which amounts to no more than saying that you and I have knowledge of each other, and we both have knowledge of him and her, and we are both known by him and her. This knowledge which people have of each other is different from the knowledge, available to us all, of the world in which we live.

There seems to be no problem about our knowledge of boots nor of the feet that go in them. But equally there seems nothing about such knowledge which distinguishes it from knowledge of the physical world. Was it not on the basis of information of this sort, a footprint in the sand, that Robinson Crusoe con-cluded that someone had been around? The problem seems to be that no evidence we could stumble across on the beach, or anywhere else in the world, could be evidence that a person was telling their own stories or acting according to their con-science, or responsible for their own actions. It is not that we have evidence for the physical aspects of personhood but not for the psychological. Stevenson is saying that despite his own experience as a writer and his reflections upon that experience, he still doesn't know where his stories come from; he is not sure whether he or some demon is responsible for them.

Philosophical doubts about the possibility of personal knowledge reflect the anxieties about the possibility of personal communication which are frequently expressed in modern liter-ature.

> 'Beatrice.'
> 'Mm?'
> 'What is it like to be you?'...
> 'Just ordinary.'...
> 'No. Tell me...Where do you live, Beatrice...Don't move. No, silly girl, not your address. Inside. The side of my head is against the side of yours. Do you live in there? We can't be an inch apart. I live near the back of my head right inside – nearer the back than the front. Are you like that? Do you live – just in here? If I put my fingers there on the nape of your neck and move them up am I close? Closer?'
>
> (Golding, 1959, pp. 103-5)

Even at moments of greatest intimacy we remain an inch apart. That inch is a chasm. It guarantees the ultimate distinctness of persons and threatens the possibility of communication. Golding's image is of a self, distinct and strong, but isolated a couple of inches behind the eyes. There is something important and valuable there to be known, but access to it is blocked. However, if access, as a matter of principle, is permanently blocked, a more sceptical thinker may transfer his anxieties, which had centred on the possibility of communication, to the very existence of the person to be communicated with. He may begin to wonder whether anything really exists behind the phenomena there to be seen. It may appear that there is little to choose between saying that there is no knowledge of persons and saying there are no persons. Both options have been explored. Our concern is not with solipsism – the view that I alone exist. The scepticism about the personal that concerns us focuses not on the existence of others, but on those qualities, including autonomy and responsibility, which are attributed to others precisely as persons.

rejections of personal knowledge

Many say that what passes as personal knowledge, in so far as it is genuinely *knowledge*, turns out to be knowledge of something other than persons; and others say that, in so far as it is genuinely *personal*, personal knowledge turns out to be something other than knowledge. In either case, the possibility of personal knowledge is denied. Some examples of these rejections of personal knowledge are represented in the diagram.

The first three isms all claim, though for different reasons, that what counts as personal knowledge turns out to be indistinguishable from our knowledge of the impersonal world.

Psychologism analyses our knowledge of persons into knowledge of psychological states, ultimately, the data of introspection, conceived of as privately accessible objects. David Hume's celebrated remarks about personal identity illustrate the point:

...nor have we any idea of *self*, after the manner it is here explained. For, from what impression could this idea be derived?...It must be some one impression that gives rise to every real idea. But self or person is not any one impression, but that to which our several impressions and ideas are supposed to have a reference.

(Hume, 1951, p. 238)

On this view the self is not an object of knowledge but some sort of imaginative construct out of the psychological states of which we do have knowledge.

Behaviourism continues the move away from the personal in its attempts to capture psychological states and functions in objective descriptions of observable behaviour. This progression is necessary because psychologism had not gone far enough. Its reliance on private data betrays objectivity. In the name of empiricism, the self had been rejected as an entity because the ego, at least as conceived by Descartes, could not possibly be an object of knowledge. According to behaviourists,

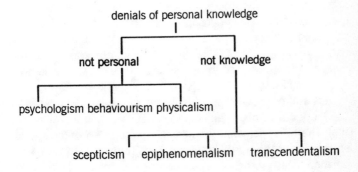

Figure 1 Diagram of the rejections of personal knowledge

knowledge had been brought no closer by substituting for the essentially unknowable self, essentially private psychological states. Knowledge is transmittable. It can be put in books and stored in computers, and lost there. It can be acquired and communicated. The fact that psychological states are accessible in principle to one person alone makes them unsuitable foundations for genuine knowledge.

Physicalism is the most thorough-going impersonalism. It is dissatisfied with behaviourism, because, it suspects, the concept of behaviour turns out to be a Trojan horse concealing mental concepts. Consequently, it aims to substitute descriptions of brain states for personal knowledge. Physicalism represents the logical consequence of the push for objectivity. What purports to be knowledge of persons is interpreted as knowledge of neurophysiological systems.

These three rejections of personal knowledge hold that what passes as personal knowledge is knowledge alright, but systematically misinterpreted knowledge, because it claims to have as its object something, which, if it were to exist at all, could not be an object of knowledge.

The following positions end up with the same rejection, but do so via a different route. Since the sixteenth century when Descartes remodelled philosophy around sceptical questions, it has been difficult, embarrasingly difficult, to explain how we can have knowledge of other people's thoughts, intentions and feelings. There seemed to be a strong contrast between knowledge of self and knowledge of others. Self-knowledge is the perfect sort of knowledge. Knowledge of others is impossible.

Scepticism about personal knowledge begins by allowing that there is personal knowledge distinct from scientific knowledge of the world, but it proceeds to restrict it to the first person. This restriction is a consequence of the belief that self-consciousness is the only knowledge of the genuinely personal. The identification of personal knowledge with first person knowledge eventually threatens its status as knowledge. If personal knowledge is restricted to our own states, there seems little difference between having an experience and knowing one is having it. Indeed, what makes first person knowledge

impregnable, is the running together of experience and know-ledge. But the price of this impregnability is incommunicability.

Thomas Nagel asks the stimulating question 'What is it like to be a bat?' One tempting response is that only a bat knows what it is like to be a bat, because knowing this involves having bat experiences. Just as knowing what baked beans taste like is to taste them or to remember tasting them. This answer equates knowledge and experience and, in so doing, implies scepticism about the possibility of acquiring knowledge of experience other than one's own. In this way, 'other mind sceptics' believe there is a dimension to personal experience which cannot be captured in objective knowledge. What began as perfect knowledge, now appears so immediately personal, in the sense of intrinsically first personal, that it could not be knowledge. It is this impasse that Wittgenstein has in mind when he writes:

> It can't be said of me at all (except perhaps as a joke) that I *know* I am in pain. What is it supposed to mean – except perhaps that I *am* in pain?

> Other people cannot be said to learn of my sensations *only* from my behaviour, – for *I* cannot be said to learn of them. I *have* them.
>
> (Wittgenstein, 1963, §246)

Epiphenomenalism is not a word on everybody's lips. It is nevertheless the name of a view that is widespread among scientifically minded thinkers. Subjective experience, it is claimed, is not real. It makes some sort of appearance, and so has some status as a phenomenon. But it is both irrelevant and illusory. It is irrelevant because it does not enter into any causal relationships with, or in any other way impinge on, the real world. It is illusory in the sense that its occurrence is restricted entirely to the domain of the subjective and perspectival, so that it has no reality which requires an explanation other than the explanation of the physical realities of which it is an epiphenomenon. What motivates this theory is the tacit assumption of much recent analytic philosophy:

> ...unless there is some way to eliminate mental phenomena, naively construed, we will be left with a class of entities that lies outside of the realm of serious science and with an impossible problem of relating these entities to the real world of physical objects.
>
> (Searle, 1983, p. 263)

Transcendentalism is a view associated with Kant. It finds a twentieth-century formulation in Wittgenstein's *Tractatus Logico-Philosophicus*. The foundation of this view is that a person could not be a phenomenon in the world. Nothing that could appear in the world we experience could be a person nor a manifestation of a person. Consequently, if persons exist, they must lie, somehow or other, outside of the experiencable environment. As Wittgenstein put it in the *Tractatus Logico-Philosophicus*:

> If I wrote a book called *The World as I Found it*, I should have to include a report on my body, and should have to say which parts were subordinate to my will, and which were not, etc., this being a method of isolating the subject, or rather of showing that in an important sense there is no subject; for it alone could *not* be mentioned in that book.

> The philosophical self is not the human being, not the human body, or the human soul, with which psychology deals, but rather the metaphysical subject, the limit of the world – not a part of it.
>
> (Wittgenstein, 1961, §5.631 & §5.641)

The previous positions we have looked at hold that the person, for one reason or another, falls beneath the level of serious attention. The Kantian axis puts forward the opposite view: the person transcends the limits of our worldly attention. Though the spirit and inspiration are very different, the upshot is the same: the person is not a possible object of knowledge.

self-expression

Rejecting all these views involves defending the opposite claim that personal knowledge is a distinctive sort of knowledge, structurally different from knowledge of the impersonal. If there is personal knowledge, then persons must become available to be known. Somehow there must be evidence that entitles us to claim personal knowledge. As we have seen, the rejections of personal knowledge are often founded on the denial of the possibility of persons manifesting themselves in the world. Thus a Cartesian 'other minds' sceptic believes that each person is an object of knowledge available through introspection to themselves, but not to others. A Humean believes that persons could not be objects of knowledge even for themselves. A transcendentalist concludes, from the impossibility of empirical evidence for the existence of persons, that persons are realities of a different order from the knowable objects of experience.

There is a need for an explanation of how so many theorists have come to deny personal knowledge. It seems inadequate to account for it in terms of a response to sceptical conundrums. Stanley Cavell in his intriguing study, 'Between Acknowledgement and Avoidance', connects what he calls 'soul-blindness' to

> an attempt to account for, and protect, our separateness, our unknowingness, our unwillingness or incapacity either to know or be known.
>
> (Cavell, 1979, pp. 329-496)

In the *Philosophical Investigations* Wittgenstein locates the source of the problem of other minds in the neglect of expression or the tendency to think of expression as evidence, on the basis of which more or less secure inferences are made.

To appreciate how expression provides the basis for personal knowledge, it is best to take easily accessible examples. The central cases of expression occur in direct communications between one person and another, in stating one's opinions, or showing one's affection or irritation, in apologising, in owning up, in blaming, or in inviting someone to dinner. If, however, we want examples which we can discuss, and pass from hand to hand, we need instances of expression in a more permanent form than a personal conversation. For this reason, literature provides a starting point. What we lose in immediacy and directness, we gain in accessibility.

A species of expression is self-expression; and a literary species of self-expression is the confession. Literary confessions are doubtless different from courtroom confessions in many ways, but there are also similaritites. Two classic examples of self-expression are the *Confessions* of St. Augustine and Rousseau. These books are intimate autobiographies. Autobiographies are not confessions in the narrow legal sense of admitting guilt. Raising your hand to own up is not a statement about yourself. The last exchange between Othello and Iago, in Act 5, Scene 2, contains an admission of guilt, at least by implication, and a refusal to confess:

> *Othello*: ...Will you, I pray, demand that demi-devil
> Why he hath thus ensar'd my soul and body?
> *Iago*: Demand me nothing. What you know, you know.
> From this time forth I never will speak word.

Nonetheless literary confessions are as close to legal confessions as they are to either the memoirs of the old soldier who sets out to recall a particular campaign and his part in it, or to the reminiscences of the elderly statesman who writes about, for example, what Lloyd George was like. Recollections of these sorts concentrate on the events and personalities of the past. Confessions are autobiographies in the most direct sense. They are self-disclosures.

confession and autonomy

In writing his autobiography Augustine thought of himself as undertaking a thoroughly moral enterprise. He presents his *Confessions* as a search for a spiritual cure. His ultimate objective is redemption through the forgiveness of his sins. Moral considerations affect not only his objectives but the confessional enterprise itself. He was aware that the main obstacle to candid self-revelation is the opacity of the human personality.

> ...I cannot understand all that I am. This means, then, that the mind is too narrow to contain itself entirely. But where is that part of it which it does not itself contain? Is it somewhere outside itself and not within it? How, then, can it be part of it, if it is not contained in it?
>
> (Augustine, 1986, Bk. 10, §8, p. 216)

Insight into the obscure depths of the individual personality can only be acquired by searching for the true self. Such knowledge is ultimately a gift received from the hands of God.

> ...as long as I am away from you, during my pilgrimage, I am more aware of myself than of you...
> I shall therefore confess both what I know of myself and what I do not know. For even what I know about myself I only know because your light shines upon me; and what I do not know about myself I shall continue not to know until I see you face to face and *my dusk is noonday*.
>
> (Augustine, 1986, Bk. 10, §5, p. 211)

During his sinful youth his energies were dissipated. Later, Augustine, the redeemed narrator, is recollected. Thus he finds a unified voice in which to make his confession. In order to make a candid confession one must overcome the temptations to lie or misrepresent the truth. But in order to lie or misrepresent one must first be able to express the truth. We must distinguish the question 'How do we know if this confession is candid?' from the question 'What are the conditions required for a candid confession to be possible?' The possibility of confession involves the autonomy of the confessant. He must be in a position to speak for himself. The fundamental obstacle to confession is the dissipation and self-deceit that results from sin.

The connection between self-expression, personal knowledge and individual autonomy is explicitly made by Augustine at the end of his account of learning to speak as an infant. (This is the end of the passage unfairly criticized at the beginning of Wittgenstein's *Investigations*)

> So, by hearing words arranged in various phrases and constantly repeated, I gradually pieced together what they stood for, and when my tongue had mastered the pronunciation, I began to express my wishes by means of them. In this way I made my wants known to my family and they made theirs known to me, and I took a further step into the stormy life of human society, although I was still subject to the authority of my parents and the will of my elders.
>
> (Augustine, 1986, Bk. 1, §8, p. 29)

Here Augustine ties together expressing his own wishes, acquiring knowledge of the wishes of others and being accepted as a person in his own right in the family. The implication is that one cannot express oneself or acquire knowledge of others without being accepted into the social relationships of a group. Wittgenstein overlooks this aspect of Augustine's remarks when he accuses him of representing language learning as if the pre-linguistic child was already an accepted member of a linguistic community, only not this one:

> ...as if the child came into a strange country and did not understand the language of the country; that is, as if it already had a language, only not this one.
>
> (Wittgenstein, 1963, §32)

Like Augustine, Rousseau sees confession as a function of autonomy. On Judgement Day he will tell God:

> 'Here is what I have done, and if by chance I have used some immaterial embellishment it has been only to fill a void due to defect of memory. I may have taken for fact what was no more than probability, but I have never put down as true what I knew to be false.'
>
> (Rousseau, 1985, p. 17)

This is autonomy in a minimal sense, which affords sufficient self-knowledge for one to guarantee that one has not told a deliberate lie about oneself. It says nothing about whether one is in a position to tell the truth about oneself.

Rousseau's concern with autonomy is less tortured than Augustine's partly because he represents a more modern sense of confession, according to which it means 'letting it all hang out'. St. Augustine saw the world, the flesh and the devil, or rather their myriad effects in the soul of man, as formidable obstacles to sincere confession. Rousseau thought that the principal obstacle was one's sense of the ridiculous, which seems to expand as one's sense of guilt diminishes.

> It is the ridiculous and the shameful, not one's criminal actions, that it is hardest to confess.
>
> (Rousseau, 1985, p. 28)

Rousseau claims that his autobiography 'has no precedent, and...once completed, will have no imitator' because other people, out of shame, are unable to achieve the total honesty and suspension of inhibitions which the task involves. He uses strong images to represent the aggressive self-revelation which he sees as part of his unique personality:

> The true object of my confession is to reveal my inner thoughts exactly in all the situations of my life. It is the history of my soul that I have promised to recount.
>
> (Rousseau, 1985, p. 262)

All Rouseau believes he has to do to put himself in a position to tell his story is to 'enter again into my inner self'. This inner world is invisible to his reader, until he can say 'I have bared my secret soul' (Rousseau, 1985, p. 262). Confession makes a person transparent. It is only to an extreme introvert like Rousseau that personal transparency could seem an ideal. The desire for personal knowledge is not a desire for transparency either in ourselves or in others. The nightmare of that idea consists not just in loss of privacy. Like animals in a cage we would have no corner to hide from the gaze of others. The more fundamental deprivation is loss of autonomy. A transparent person is passive. Others would only have to look into you to see what you thought and felt. Our desire for knowledge of others can only be satisfied by free and authoritative self-revelation. This is because unless it is free and authoritative it is not the revelation of a person.

The image of transparency suggests another problem about autobiographies and the truth. Transparency suggests that the role of the self-revealer is simply to draw aside the veil. The suspicion about autobiographies is that the story-teller does more than simply reveal, he creates an image. However, if transparency is recognised as a pseudo-ideal, then the very conditions for telling your own story need not be seen as threats to the truth of that story.

Thomas Addison in his essay 'Friendship' talks of self-expression in the active terms with which the ideal of transparency is incompatible. At the same time he reasserts the Augustinian claim that self-revelation requires a community:

> ...the most open, instructive, and unreserved discourse, is that which passes between two persons who are familiar and intimate friends. On these occasions, a man gives a loose to every passion and every thought that is uppermost, discovers his most retired opinion of persons and things, tries the beauty and strength of his sentiments, and exposes his whole soul to the examination of his friend.
>
> (Addison, 1960, pp. 48-9)

The *Confessions* of Augustine and Rousseau, indeed all auto-biographies, are works of art, self-conscious creations. They are deliberate and calculated self-presentations. They are to be judged as such. The fact that they are the product of artifice does not prevent them from being authoritative acts of self-disclosure. On the contrary, it is only if they are considered presentations that they can be assessed as self-portraits. A confession cannot be artless, like a cry. Even if the cry is a howl of remorse.

The insistence on the social complexity of legal confessions by Michel Foucault and those influenced by him, undermines the naive idea that even a legal admission can be interpreted as a straightforward 'owning up'. Once the structure of confessions is made explicit, it becomes impossible to maintain such a simple view of them. The reliability of confessions in criminal proceedings becomes a major problem. It may be difficult or even impossible to establish the reliability of confessions. However, they do not lose their unique status as self-disclosures because of those difficulties. To reject them in favour of some more objective source of information, would be to cut oneself off from access to personal qualities that can only be communicated through direct self-disclosure.

confessions and truthfulness

In Book 10 of the *Confessions* Augustine reflects on the implications of his autobiographical undertaking. He makes clear the moral dimensions of self-revelation, and raises the question of the truth of confessions.

> When they hear me speak about myself, how do they know whether I am telling the truth, since no one *knows a man's thoughts, except the man's own spirit that is within him?*...And if a man recognise his true self, can he possibly say 'This is false', unless he is himself a liar? But charity believes all things – all things, that is, which are spoken by those who are joined as one in charity – and for this reason I, too, O Lord, make my confession aloud in the hearing of men. For although I cannot prove to them that my confessions are true, at least I shall be believed by those whose ears are opened to me by charity.
>
> (Augustine, 1986, Bk. 10, §3, p. 208)

St. Augustine's answer to the question 'How do they know whether I am telling the truth?' is to deflect the force of the question, which, as it stands, can only be answered negatively, 'I cannot prove to them that my confessions are true.' The issue is not 'Are his statements true?', but 'Is he believable?'

St. Augustine offers his *Confessions* as genuine self-revelations. If we return to our question, how can a person be manifest in the world and so become a possible object of knowledge, his answer would be: *through confession in a community bound together through charity*.

Rousseau's *Confessions* are a thoroughly secular undertaking. He does, nonetheless, imagine himself before the Divine Throne, book in hand, not quaking before the Sovereign Judge, but calling on God as a witness to his veracity. This egomanical fantasy illustrates that what the confessant needs is a witness to his truthfulness, not evidence for the truth of his reports.

Wittgenstein makes this point explicitly in the *Philosophical Investigations:*

> The criteria for the truth of the *confession* that I thought such-and-such are not the criteria for a true *description* of a process. And the importance of the true confession does not reside in its being a correct and certain report of a process. It resides rather in the special consequences which can be drawn from a confession whose truth is guaranteed by the special criteria of *truthfulness*.

(Wittgenstein, 1963, §222)

The truthfulness of the confessant is not the best we can do in the absence of any proof of the truth of the confession. The two are different considerations and their difference brings out one important difference between the structure of self-expressions and objective statements about the world.

When Wittgenstein is reflecting on the nature of expressions – in fact expressions of pain – he makes the following remark:

> 'When I say "I am in pain" I am at any rate justified *before myself*.' What does that mean? Does it mean: 'If someone else could know what I am calling "pain", he would admit that I was using the the word correctly'?
> To use a word without justification does not mean to use it without right.

(Wittgenstein, 1963, §289)

Part of what Wittgenstein means is that when we express our sensations, feelings or thoughts, what is at stake is our *right* to speak for ourselves. What is fundamental is not the truth of what we say nor the evidence that could be produced in support, but our authority to speak for ourselves.

To adduce evidence for one's confession is to present one's confessional statement as an objective report which needs to be and could be supported by evidence, more or less strong. Of course, a confession can be shown to be false by contradictory evidence. A confession can be corroborated by the facts. But an appeal to corroboration has a price. It forces one's confidants to withdraw from the confessional exchange and adopt an incompatible role as objective assessors of evidence. The confessor becomes the detective. It destroys the distinctive status of the confession. It implies that one has lost confidence in one's role as a confessant. This loss of confidence may flow from one's own lack of candour, but it could equally be the consequence of the withdrawal of an unsympathetic listener.

Suppose a parent asks a child if it has taken the small change missing from the mantlepiece. The child denies it. If the parent expresses scepticism and withholds acceptance of the child's statement, the child may say, 'Search me. Turn out my pockets and look through my drawers.' This does not strengthen the child's position, it expresses weakness. The child is saying, 'I despair of having my word accepted, of being, myself, accepted. So look to the facts.' If the evidence bears out the child's original statement, the standard reaction is not satisfaction that conclusive proof has been unearthed, but recrimination that trust was undermined.

Stanley Cavell makes a similar point in reference to a truth serum:

> When I felt I had to get to the other's sensation apart from his giving expression to it (as if that were the way to ensure certainty, or as if the way to insure his candidness was to prevent *his* playing any role in his expression) my wish was to penetrate his behaviour with my reference to his sensation, in order to reach the same spot *his* reference to himself occupies *before*, so to speak, the sensation gets expressed. (We might think of the effect of a truth serum as preventing someone's playing a role in his expression. But we will not think of this as his speaking candidly.)
>
> (Cavell, 1979, p. 342)

If an accused person volunteers to be injected with a so-called truth serum, is he attempting to produce evidence of the truth of his confessions or is he offering to put himself in a position in which his candour is guaranteed? There seems to be a paradox. On the one hand, the procedure seems based on the assumption that 'the way to to insure his candidiness was to prevent his playing any role in his expression'; on the other, if the drugged person has no control over his expressions, 'we will not think of this as his speaking candidly'. The problem is that a truth serum aims to guarantee candour, but it does so by undermining autonomy which is a principal condition of candour.

confession and spontaneity
Rousseau does not share St. Augustine's anxiety about the confessional enterprise because, on the whole, the undertaking seemed to him comparatively easy:

> I may omit or transpose facts, or make mistakes in dates; but I cannot go wrong about what I have felt, or about what my feelings have led me to do; and these are the chief subjects of my story. It is the history of my soul that I have promised to recount, and to write it faithfully I have need of no other memories; it is enough if I enter again into my inner self, as I have done till now.
>
> (Rousseau, 1985, Bk. 7, p. 262)

Nevertheless, Rousseau recognised the difficulties of writing his confessions. He had to penetrate behind the socially compromised man to produce 'a portrait in every way true to nature'. His book was undertaken in a context of pressure and tension. It was the more or less forced response to accusations of debauchery that Voltaire had levelled at him. Though he may not have been tortured by guilt and the fear of damnation, his confessions were anything but the product of indifference.

This allows us to make a final point about self-expression as exhibited in these *Confessions*. Though a confession has to be spontaneous and freely made, it is never idly made. One may betray oneself in an idle moment, give oneself away, let slip a clue to something about one. A confession, on the other hand, is a deliberate act of self-revelation, but it is one made under some sort of pressure. Legal confessions are backed up by oaths. Rituals are maintained to solemnize the making of confessions. Even the perversion of torture shares this logic. Torture has been and still is used to extract confessions, not only for the obvious and cynical reason that witnesses have to be forced to say things they are unwilling to say, but also because a confession that has no element of compulsion about it is not a reliable confession. Leaving aside any other moral scruples, the trouble with torture, as with the truth serum, is that it destroys what it sets out to guarantee, the candour of the confession. In a doomed attempt to avoid destroying its own objectives, torture used to extract confessions, as opposed to torture as a punishment, was a tightly controlled procedure. Confessions extracted under torture had to be 'freely' repeated in court. Of course, we reject these efforts to legitimize cruelty. We are suspicious of confessions made under serious pressure and we discount those extracted by torture. Nevertheless, confessions would not be confessions unless they were in some sense forced.

The sort of pressure or difficulty that accompanies confessions is social. It consists of two elements, a certain reluctance and a degree of necessity. Legal confessions are considered reliable evidence of guilt on the assumption that, as a confession is against self-interest, it would only be made if it were true. This may be a naive view, but it recognises the point being made here, that an act of self-disclosure is only a confession if there are factors which tend to inhibit it. This is true not only in criminal cases where the consequences of confession are obvious. The autobiographies of Augustine and Rousseau are called *Confessions* in part to capture this sense of difficult and reluctant self-exposure. We lose faith in the 'confessions' of starlets in the tabloid press, when we realise that their revelations are hawked about by tireless publicity agents.

In tension with this reluctance is the necessity to confess. If one feels no compulsion to reveal oneself, if what one says about oneself is said with the same indifference as a remark about the weather, then, whatever one has done, one has not confessed. The pressure to confess comes from the need for acknowledgement and acceptance. In the case of crime or sin this acceptance is attainable only through forgiveness.

We have then at the heart of confession, which is one, though only one, of the most intimate forms of self-expression, a tension between the requirements of spontaneity and of pressure. Wittgenstein noticed this feature of expressive language when he wrote:

> In this way I should like to say the words 'Oh, *let* him come!'
> are charged with my desire. And words can be wrung from us,
> – like a cry. Words can be *hard* to say: such, for example, as
> are used to effect a renunciation, or to confess a weakness.
> (Words are also deeds.)

(Wittgenstein, 1963, §546)

confession and personal knowledge

The purpose of these remarks about the *Confessions* of Augustine and Rousseau was to discover in what way confession, as an example of self-expression, could supply us with genuine knowledge of persons. We have seen that many groups of philosophers have denied the possibility of such knowledge. They find it impossible, for different reasons, to allow that persons could appear in the world and so be objects of knowledge. They believe, depending on their respective positions, that bodies, brains, behaviour patterns, or mental states were available objects of knowledge, and knowledge of these was either equivalent to, or would afford the best substitute for, knowledge of persons.

Confessions illustrate how self-expression can play the role for personal knowledge that data plays for objective knowledge of the environment. For another way of stating the problem posed by those who are sceptical of personal knowledge would be: persons cannot be data. But in confessions, and in many other less formal ways, people make themselves available, and give themselves over to be known.

The issue of the reliablity of confessions must be kept separate from questions about the nature of confessions. We must distinguish between how we can know that a confession is truthful, and what it is about a confession that enables it to communicate personal truths. There is no guarantee that a confession is genuine, any more than there is an assurance that avowals are sincere or statements true. This does not allow in an indefinite scepticism about other minds. The lack of a guarantee highlights what is a plain fact of life that personal knowledge is not based on foundations of certainty. The resolution of scepticism about other minds lies not in basic, unquestionable truths but in mutual acceptance in a common life.

If we reflect on the nature of, and the conditions for, confessions, serious obstacles arise in the way of our accepting anything the psychopath says as a genuine confession. If this is the case then the main avenue to mutual understanding is closed down. Incomprehension and rejection are inevitable.

Confession involves presenting and explaining oneself, in a context where there is some difficulty or obstacle to acceptance. It is a search for acknowledgement, acceptance, and sometimes forgiveness. A confession cannot be totally spontaneous, like a cry, because it is, among other things, an invitation to reconstruct our relationships. The confessant must be autonomous, having the authority to speak for himself to others in a shared world. Therefore, he cannot be lost in illusion or self-deceit. Only relatively good people can make confessions.

On all counts there are difficulties, which suggests that extreme depravity brings in its wake a separateness and isolation which in our culture we express most naturally in the language of insanity.

notes

Our remarks about confessions relied on the autobiographical writings of St. Augustine and Jean-Jacques Rousseau.

St. Augustine (354-430), the greatest of the Church Fathers, was the dominant influence on religious thought until the Reformation. His work *The City of God* had a profound influence on the development of views concerning the relationship between the spiritual and secular aspects of life. His *Confessions* are an intimate record of his escape from what he saw as a sinful past into a life of faith.

Jean-Jacques Rousseau (1712-78), a political and social philosopher, saw a conflict between the needs of a dynamic human nature and the artificial restraints that society imposes. This tension he detects in both political and personal spheres. His *Confessions* are, in part, a justification of his own natural virtue in the face of the misrepresentation and persecution which, he believed, were directed against him because of his social nonconformity and the uniqueness of his personality.

In this chapter, I am especially indebted to the enigmatic but highly suggestive writings of the American philosopher Stanley Cavell. His treatment of the problem of 'Other Minds' can be found in:
Cavell, S., 1979, *Claims of Reason* (Oxford, Clarendon, N.Y., OUP).

The other books to which reference is made are:
Addison, 1960, *Essays from Addison* (London, MacMillan, N.Y., St. Martin's Press).
Saint Augustine, 1986, *Confessions* (Harmondsworth, Penguin Books).
Golding, W., 1959, *Free Fall* (London, Faber and Faber).
Hume, D., 1951, *A Treatise of Human Nature*, vol. 1 (London, Dent).
Rousseau. J.-J., 1985, *Confessions* (Harmondsworth, Penguin Books).
Searle, J., 1983, *Intentionality* (London, N.Y., Cambridge University Press).
Stevenson, R.L., 1987, *Dr Jekyll and Mr Hyde and Weir of Hermiston* (Oxford, N.Y., OUP).
Wittgenstein, L., 1961, *Tractatus Logico-Philosophicus,* trans. D.F. Pears and B.F. McGuinness (London, Routledge and Kegan Paul).
Wittgenstein, L., 1963, *Philosophical Investigations*, trans, G.E.M. Anscombe (Oxford, Blackwell).

7: morality and gross depravity

two aspects of evil

From ancient times an analogy has been drawn between physical and spiritual health. Goodness is the well-being of the soul; wickedness is a spiritual illness. The notion of total physical sickness is, not surprisingly, absurd. Anyone who is totally physically sick is dead, and therefore not sick. Is there not a similar absurdity involved in the idea of total spiritual sickness? Someone who approximates to the limit of total depravity or malice is morally dead. Whatever about the analogy, problems arise when we attempt to extend our moral judgements and reactions to extreme cases. David Parkin claims that our talk of evil has a dual purpose:

> ...there are two very important strands to our way of thinking about evil: in addition to the sense of evil as something which is against the rules of social conduct, there is also the view that the concept of evil is always in the making, with no fixed positions from which to define it, nor set corners in which to place it. Rather, it could be seen as a coming-together, in response to an event, of a group of people's emotions of anger, horror, despair, and disbelief.
>
> (Babuta and Bragard, 1988, p. 24)

Concern for social order and intimations of moral horror do not sit easily together. The former does not naturally develop into the latter as the offences become more serious. On the contrary, the two aspects of evil demand quite different responses. Systems of criminal law are elaborate structures of procedures for determining guilt and distributing punishments on a proportional basis. There are complicated rules about excuses and mitigations. The purpose of any system of criminal law is to arrive at a definite decision on any matter that comes before it in a limited period of time. The inherently unstructured sense of horror and outrage that is part of our sense of evil can never be adequately expressed or represented in legal procedures. The wail of the Greek chorus cannot be contained in a legal judgement.

Barbara Wootton sees in the inability to apply ordinary moral concepts to the worst cases, an indication of the incoherence of the whole moral system and of the concept of responsibility in particular. If we hold back from ascribing responsibility in the cases of gross depravity, we betray our unease about the whole moral business:

> ...if you are consistently (in old-fashioned language) wicked enough, you may hope to be excused from responsibility for your misdeeds; but if your wickedness is only moderate, or if you show occasional signs of repentance and reform, then you must expect to take the blame for what you do and perhaps also to be punished for it.
>
> So illogical a position can hardly, one would think, prove tenable for long. Hence the psychopath may well prove to be the thin end of the wedge which will ultimately shatter the whole idea of moral responsibility...

> (Wootton, 1959, pp. 250-1)

This is a weak argument. The non-applicability of the limiting concept in no way inclines us to deny that it makes sense to talk about people being more or less wicked, as they can be more or less sick. Nor are we inclined to take sickness any the less seriously because we can never say of anyone that they are totally sick.

What can have led Baronness Wootton to believe that the psychopath is central rather than, as I am suggesting, peripheral to the concepts of responsibility? Perhaps she thinks that morality claims to regulate the relations between people and that if it equips us to do anything, it ought to equip us to deal easily and readily with the cases in which those relationships have gone wrong in the most serious way and on the largest scale. It is implausible, however, to suggest that if we feel uncertain in our attitude towards Eichmann and Sutcliffe, we should feel equally insecure when we return home and tell our children not to be cruel or selfish or mean. Morality begins at home. Our moral vocabulary trips off the tongue most easily when we are dealing with children or friends in domestic matters. We begin to feel a slight hesitancy in the office, or at a political meeting, and we stutter on the battlefield. Of course we must maintain our efforts to extend our moral behaviour into a wider and wider world. But we should not imagine that this is an easy task, which has only to be held up as an ideal to be achieved.

punishing evil

Judges are inclined to denounce the criminal as they pronounce sentence. Their remarks tend to be noticed only when they plumb new depths of judicial prejudice or eccentricity. Even remarks that are not blatantly inappropriate seem, in the case of gross crime, to be uncomfortable and beside the point. It is one thing to remonstrate with someone who is guilty of some dishonesty or recklessness or hooliganism, and another to admonish someone whose whole way of life manifests his insensitivity to the moral order. If a judge is sending a man to prison for life, there is little purpose in offering the opinion that he is a very bad person. As Mr. Justice Boreham sentenced Peter Sutcliffe to life imprisonment, with a recommendation that he serve at least thirty years, he offered the following thought:

> The jury have found you guilty of thirteen charges of murder, if I may say so, murder of a very cowardly nature. For each was a woman.

> (Yallop, 1981, p. 361)

We may wonder if there is a brave way of hitting total strangers with a hammer. It is not just flippancy that suggests the question: would we think more of Sutcliffe had he chosen men as targets? Would his crimes be less serious had he given his victims a chance to resist? The problem with the judge's comments is not one of taste. Any moral discourse seems inappropriate. This suggests that the disposal of such criminals cannot be read as normal punishment.

We have argued that being responsible is not the same thing as being liable to punishment. Nonetheless in criminal matters, if punishment is inappropriate then the notion of responsibility is also in jeopardy. The nature and justification of punishment are contentious issues to which there is no widely accepted solution. Punishments ought to produce, or at least aim to produce, some social benefit by way of deterrence or reform. But, most philosophers believe, the pursuit of social advantage must be qualified by considerations which refer to the wrong-doer. Any particular punishment must relate to what the offender deserves; it must fit the crime; it must reinstate the offender; we must be able honestly to consider it to be an expression of moral concern and indignation. In all of these respects the attempt to punish the grossly depraved runs into insuperable difficulties.

What punishment fits the gross crimes we are considering? Hannah Arendt, in her famous study of the Eichmann trial, considers some of the anomalies that arise in relation to punishing the crimes of the Holocaust. She refers to 'the fearsome, word-and-thought-defying *banality of evil*' (Arendt, 1963, p. 231). The banality lay in the thoughts and feelings that motivated the man who organised the death of millions. He may not have been a demonic personality, but however banal his character, his crimes were anything but banal. The alleged ordinariness of his personality does not make his offences ordinary nor give us a licence to treat him as if he was an ordinary criminal. The special dimensions of the crimes that Eichmann was involved in become apparent in the issue of punishment. This was recognised as a problem at the time of the trial. Arendt comments:

> The most common argument (against executing Eichmann) was that Eichmann's deeds defied the possibility of human punishment, that it was pointless to impose the death sentence for crimes of such magititude – which, of course, was true, in a sense, except that it could not conceivably mean that he who

had murdered millions should for this very reason escape punishment.

(Arendt, 1963, pp. 228-9)

The sense in which normal penal calculations fail is in terms of the gravity of the punishment which should be in proportion to the crime. It seems impossible to make such a calculation when the victims are to be counted in millions. Arendt is sensitive to this thought, but remains firm in her conviction that it should make no difference. It would be absurd if Eichmann were not punished; and even more absurd if the reason for his immunity were the number of his victims. Arendt underestimates the difficulty. If we cannot calculate due proportion in relation to punishment, the very notion of punishment is at risk.

In soccer, for example, there is a series of punishments that a referee can impose on a team and on individual players. They vary in severity and are supposed to be imposed in relation to the gravity of the offence. If a referee would award a penalty kick and send off the offending player for punching an opponent in his own penalty area, what punishment should he impose were the defender to produce a machine gun and mow down the opposition? The rules of soccer cannot accommodate such an offence. No doubt the contest would stop and the game be awarded to the team whose players had been assassinated, assuming that what was left of the team continued to play in the league. But this is not a penalty imposed within the game. It marks the point at which soccer, with its rules and penalties, came to an end. Even if one could produce some semblance of a penal calculus, would one want to? And if one wanted to, would it be a punishment? We could write a rule that covered the deliberate killing of one's sporting opponent. There are already such rules, but they are not, and could not be rules of soccer. They are rules of the criminal law which govern what you are allowed to get away with as part of 'manly sport'. The question is: does the criminal law have limits just as there are limits to the application of the laws of soccer? The answer to this question may seem to be a straightforward 'No'. The criminal law, unlike the rules of a sport, has to cover all conceivable action. It must supply an appropriate penalty for any conceivable offence. The law governs every aspect of a citizen's life whereas the rules of a particular sport cover only the participants in relation to this one activity.

Nevertheless it is possible to doubt the omnicompetence of the criminal law. In soccer there is a limit to the severity of penalties that can be imposed within the game. Is the same true in the case of the law? One indication that there is a limit to judicial punishment is the fact that the degree of punishment that seems to be called for in the worst cases conflicts with other requirements of a decent and defensible penal system. Foucault's study of punishment concentrates on the penalties for the most serious of crimes, treason and regicide. Barbaric punishments were devised as proportionate responses to offences against political authority which was thought to have a divine legitimacy. The result was an orgy of cruelty that is quite indefensible as part of a penal system. We cannot hang, draw and quarter someone and see it as an expression of moral concern. It is not that awful punishment conflicts with other values we may wish to uphold. The tension is internal to any notion of punishment that retains a minimal recognition of the moral status of the criminal. We can try – if we are so inclined – to justify imposing awful fates on criminals on the same sort of grounds we might use to justify acts of war, but we ought not to dress up our actions in the language of retributive punishment. There is no room in moral exchanges for terrible punishments. The acceptance of extreme penalties is a corruption that results from the attempt to maintain penal practices up to the limits of evil.

Eternal damnation is a theological example of punishment at the limit. Fortunately it is not a punishment that human beings are in any position to impose on each other. As regards punishment in the next life, human ingenuity is restricted to working out theories which claim to justify it. St. Thomas Aquinas, who believed that some people merit damnation, realised that to make sense of this doctrine he had to do two things. First he must explain the damnable malice of the sin. This he does by arguing that the malice results solely from the object of the offence, namely God Himself. Secondly he must retain the moral status even of those in Hell, which is why he insists on what he calls the 'natural goodness' of the damned. This natural goodness consists of rationality and 'the seeds of intellectual and moral virtues' present in anyone who is rational.

Aquinas realises that he must maintain these two positions at the same time. Even he has problems. At one point, for example, he quotes St. Gregory with approval: 'The wicked would like to live forever so that they could continue forever in their iniquities' (*Summa Theologiae*, 1a 2ae 87, 4). A formula like this has the advantage of explaining the malice of sin and its damnable nature. It is indeed hard to see what even an omnipotent and all-merciful God could do with someone who seriously willed to sin everlastingly. On the other hand, the formula is difficult to reconcile with the retention of rationality and the inclination to virtue that must characterise the sinner. Aquinas creates this dilemma because he has lapsed moment-arily from the view that the extreme malice of mortal sin arises from the object of the offence. He has been tempted to try a non-theological explanation in terms of the subjective state of the sinner. The apparent coherence of the doctrine of damn-ation can be maintained only as long as one's eye is firmly fixed on another world. As soon as the contingencies that surround all human action, even the most malicious, are allowed to intrude, the idea becomes ridiculous.

Further gruesome medieval light is cast on the limits of punishment by another aspect of Aquinas' theory of damnation. As the punishment envisaged includes not only fire but the sense of loss experienced by the creature forever separated from its final end, it is not only unjust to damn a person who is not a moral agent, it is logically impossible. Such a person, being unable to feel remorse, and experiencing no attraction towards the good, would not feel deprived by being banished from God's presence. This contains an important point: if the degree of enmity between the authority and the offender has become extreme, punishment becomes impossible. You cannot punish someone who is no good at all.

In the epilogue to her book on Eichmann, Arendt imagines

judges more candid than those who actually tried the case, condemning the accused to death in the following words:

> '...just as you supported and carried out a policy of not wanting to share the earth with the Jewish people and the people of a number of other nations – as though you and your superiors had any right to determine who should and who should not inhabit the world – we find that no one, that is, no member of the human race, can be expected to want to share the earth with you. This is the reason, and the only reason, you must hang.'
>
> (Arendt, 1963, pp. 255-6)

Whatever else is to be said of these sentiments, and there are a number of disturbing aspects to them, they do not amount to a defence of execution as a just punishment. If they suggest anything about appropriate punishment, it is that exile, rather than death, would be the way of dealing with Eichmann. Death would only be a means of insuring what is really required, namely that we no longer share the same space with him. Whether such a permanent sending to Coventry can be contemplated as a punishment is a further question.

Arendt is aware of the difficulty of her position. She locates it in the contrast between the horror of the Holocaust and the prosaic mentality of one of its leading perpetrators. She believes that some fundamental assumptions, legal and moral, have to be sacrificed if her particular defence of the execution of Eichmann is to be maintained. Because he 'commits his crimes under circumstances that make it well-nigh impossible for him to know or to feel that he is doing wrong' (Arendt, 1963, p. 253), we have to abandon, in her opinion, the fundamental assumption that 'intent to do wrong is necessary for the commission of a crime'. This remark needs clarification. 'Intent to do wrong' which is a necessary part of *mens rea* is not the same as knowing and feeling that one is doing wrong. It is a more objective test than that. Eichmann's intention was to organize the destruction of millions of people. Whatever his reasons may have been, they cannot turn that intention into a non-criminal intention.

In order for Eichmann to be condemned he must have had

a criminal intent; but in order for his intent to be criminal, it is not necessary that he thought and felt that he was doing wrong. Nothing in these remarks captures what is difficult about the Eichmann case. They apply to all criminal acts which require *mens rea*. For *mens rea* always allows the possibility of a gap opening up between subjective and objective views of the intention of the offender. Someone who shoplifts may think of himself as striking a blow for the proletariat against capitalistic consumerism. He is still guilty of theft. On any account of criminal intent, Eichmann is guilty of mass murder.

Arendt is distracted into remarking on Eichmann's intentions because she is determined to defend the execution of Eichmann whatever his intentions were. She is prepared to abandon the legal presumption that crime, almost always, involves an intention to do wrong, in order to maintain her position. In so doing she comes close to saying that she wants Eichmann executed whether he is guilty or not. In place of the requirement of criminal intent, she finds the 'supreme justification for the death penalty' in propositions which she recognizes are thought of as 'barbaric':

> ...that a great crime offends nature, so that the very earth cries out for vengeance; that evil violates a natural harmony which only retribution can restore; that a wronged collectivity owes a duty to the moral order to punish the criminal.
>
> (Arendt, 1963, p. 254)

These remarks raise the same difficulties as the language Arendt imagines being used in the ideal death sentence. The problem lies not in what is said, but the attempt to say such things in a judicial context. The convictions that Arendt expresses are unexceptionable. They belong, however, in just war theory not criminal law. In contrast with Arendt's statements, there is nothing difficult or anomalous in, for example, Churchill's explanation of his intentions towards Hitler, 'I mean beat him and his powers of evil into death, dust and ashes' (Gilbert, 1986, p. 367). His statement was not made to a court but to a nation at war; he was asking not for a particular verdict, but for an extreme effort; he was not sentencing Hitler to death, but committing himself to his destruction.

The shift from justifiable war to legal propriety was always recognised as a problem. At Yalta the leaders of the Allies discussed how war criminals ought to be treated. Ironically it was only Stalin who thought that trials ought to be held and presented no problem.

> Was it Stalin's view, Churchill asked, 'that grand criminals should be tried before being shot', in other words, that it should be a 'judicial rather than a political act'. Stalin replied that 'that was so'. But Roosevelt commented that 'it should not be too judicial'. He wanted to keep out newspapers and photographers until the criminals were dead.
>
> (Gilbert, 1986, p. 1202)

What is special about the Eichmann case, it goes without saying, is the monumental nature of the crime he committed. If there is a difficulty in handling him, it arises from this and this alone. The psychological banality of the perpetrators of the Holocaust is beside the point. It would not help if they were more flamboyant in their wickedness. We may feel happier about executing someone whose personality is offensive in a more positive way than Eichmann's, according to Arendt's understanding of him. But it does nothing to make the criminal procedures seem any more appropriate to the day in, day out, mass slaughter of the innocents that took place with such inhumanity in Auschwitz and all the other camps for which Eichmann was directly responsible.

There is a point of view, however, from which legal punishment in the case of Eichmann makes straightforward sense. The evil administrator is very different from the psychopath. He presents us with different problems and suggests different solutions. One way in which he differs is that he is affected by normal social pressures that influence us all. He could hardly have succeeded in public administration without minimum social competence. There are, consequently, unproblematic deterrent reasons for punishing Eichmann. Future bureaucrats must be persuaded that crimes they commit against humanity at the behest of their political masters may very well be punished. Bureaucrats are the sort of calculating, self-conscious agents who are capable of being deterred. If

Eichmann had thought himself subject to the authority and penalties of some system other than the Third Reich he may have acted very differently. There can be no objection in principle to the international community deciding that, in so far as different states can guarantee it, politicians and public servants who precipitate wars or who commit crimes against humanity, will be brought before an international tribunal and punished.

The practical difficulties are obvious and may make any such international scheme impossible, but they are not the real problem here. Anyone who, like Hannah Arendt, is convinced that Eichmann must die, is unlikely to be satisfied with a justification based on deterrence, even if an effective system of deterrence could be instituted. Their conviction is not based on a prudential judgement about what effect his execution may have on future generations of public servants. So though there is a respectable justification for the execution, it seems not to be the right sort of explanation; and the right sort of explanation seems not to be respectable.

We have referred to the Eichmann trial to illustrate the point that in the case of horrific crimes, legal punishment ceases to be an appropriate response. If we proceed with it, we do so only by ignoring many considerations that would normally be counted as essential requirements for just punishment. In other respects the Eichmann case is very different from the serial killings which we are considering. Legal punishment is even less appropriate in the case of the psychopath than in the case of the evil adminstrator, because even the justification in deterrence terms is unavailable. Deterrence, it is almost univ- ersally agreed, is out of the question in relation to psychopathic killings. The psychopath, unlike the evil administrator, is not affected by considerations of the fate that lies in store for him, and the non-psychopathic person does not need to be deterred from crimes that are inconceivable to him.

Just as there is no appropriate punishment in the case of the gross crimes, there is equally no point at which forgiveness becomes appropriate. A society which has rejected the death penalty, creates a problem about what to do in the long run with those who would otherwise have been executed. If we are not prepared to kill them, they must be allowed to live some sort of life. In practice this seems to require that the possibility of eventual release is never totally removed. There will come a time when parole will be considered. This implies from the moral point of view that a time will come when the record will have been put straight, when the 'debt to society' has been paid, when even those guilty of the worst crimes will be forgiven. Many people find this wholly unacceptable. The Christian commitment to the forgiveness of all sins is rejected not only by those who have special personal reasons for cultivating vengeance. Primo Levi's remarks about the unforgivable nature of the selection of prisoners for gassing in Auschwitz are not founded on his resentment at the pain he or his friends endured. They are based on more impersonal considerations.

> Does Kuhn not understand that what happened today is an abomination, which no propitiatary prayer, no pardon, no expiation by the guilty, which nothing at all in the power of man can ever clean again.

(Levi, 1987, p. 136)

Even the perpetrators can become aware that they have closed by their own acts the usual avenues of reconciliation and rehabilitation. Even a man as insensitive as Eichmann could see the fatuity of apologising. With more wisdom than perhaps he realised, he said 'Repentance is for little children' (Arendt, 1963, p. 21).

the moral world

> We now invite the reader to contemplate the possible meaning in the Lager of the words 'good' and 'evil', 'just' and 'unjust'; let everybody judge, on the basis of the picture we have outlined and of the examples given above, how much of our ordinary moral world could survive on this side of the barbed wire.

(Levi, 1987, p. 92)

Levi talks of 'our ordinary moral world' and in this book we have used the contrast between the psychopath and 'us', between the aberrant and the normal, to distinguish the community of responsible persons from those who fall outside it. There are dangers in talking in these terms. The moral world may seem like a cosy creation from which we arbitrarily exclude whatever is too uncomfortable to live with. The reference to *us* and *them* may disguise an appeal to a spurious solidarity. The moral world is not much like a geographical area, nor is being a citizen of it much like being a member of a golf club.

Talk of a moral world is metaphorical. The point of the metaphor is to emphasise the social, interpersonal nature of morality, to combat the theory that morality is constituted out of private sentiments or an inner law, and to express the idea that there are limits to moral concerns, judgements and reactions. The limits are not like the borders of a country. They are neither fixed over time, nor precise – there is, at any given moment, a significant area of uncertainty and discretion. Nevertheless they are real. One knows that the limit has been reached when moral relationships fail and moral strategies become pointless.

Primo Levi bears witness to the destruction of moral values in the world that was brought into existence in the camps. Yet there was some sort of society there. It was not just infernal chaos. The camps were institutions with their own organ- isation, routines and economies. Thousands of people worked there, and found some sort of reason for going on; many survived and millions died. Himmler could even congratulate his men in the following terms:

> ...I also want to talk to you quite frankly on a grave matter...I mean the extermination of the Jewish race...Most of you must know what it means when 100 corpses are lying side by side, or 500, or 1000. To have stuck it out and at the same time – apart from exceptions caused by human weakness – to have remained decent fellows, that is what has made us hard. This is a page of glory in our history...
> (Shirer, 1973, p. 1150)

Crimes of this degree of brutality are not so easily accom- modated in human society. Their evil effects flow out beyond the immediate harm and destruction. They shatter moral cohesion. Levi's central point is that a society can be brought into being in which it is virtually impossible for people, even those who are the innocent victims, to maintain a moral community. Himmler's claim that personal integrity can be maintained in such an environment, even by the persecutors, is a ghastly illusion. Nonetheless, the camps were societies of a sort. The serial killers with whom we are concerned could not form a society. They do not dream of building a new order. They need the old order through which they can move, dominating and destroying. The concentration camps could not exist without destroying moral life; the psychopath cannot act without cutting himself off from moral life.

However, it is easy to overstate the case. Psychopathic killers are not to be held responsible for their actions, but that does not mean that they fall outside the sphere of moral concern. There has been a tendency in European thought to base concern, which is genuinely moral concern, on rights and duties. On this view, although people, animals and the environment can be in various ways charming, amusing and attractive, it is only those who act out of principle and are, consequently, responsible agents who are worthy of respect. As a result it becomes difficult to explain why we should have obligations in relation to immature or mentally handicapped people, or to animals, let alone to the inanimate world. If the actions of morally responsible persons are the only proper objects of moral attention, then non-responsible persons fall outside the moral sphere. Their unaccountability is bought at the price of their having no moral claims on the rest of us. One of the purposes of the rhetoric which places the psychopath in the bestial category is to suggest that we owe them nothing, that they have lost all title to be treated as human beings.

In 1953 Martin Buber took the controversial step of accepting the Peace Prize of the German Book Trade in Frankfurt. He delivered a speech in which he made the essential point in reference to the Holocaust that those who cultivate cruelty can make it impossible for us to treat them as responsible beings.

> I, who am one of those who remained alive, have only in a formal sense a common humanity with those who took part in this action. They have so radically removed themselves from the human sphere, so transposed themselves into a sphere of

> monstrous inhumanity inaccessible to my conception, that not
> even hatred, much less an overcoming of hatred, was able to
> arise in me. And what am I that I could presume to 'forgive!'
> (Diamond, p. 232)

It is tempting to talk of such people in terms of losing one's soul.
But what they lose is not, as Buber's rhetoric suggests, their
humanity. They remove themselves not from the 'human
sphere' but from the society of the accountable. Buber plays
on the ambiguity of the word 'inhumanity'. The sort of inhumanity he is referring to is all too human. The psychopath
shares with us a common humanity; he remains a person. By
identifying accountability with humanity, Buber leaves himself
open to the sort of criticism Hannah Arendt voices when she
writes:

> This lofty attitude was, of course, more of a luxury than those
> who had to try Eichmann could afford, since the law pre-
> supposes precisely that we have a common humanity with
> those whom we accuse and judge and condemn.
> (Arendt, 1963, p. 253)

Of course, the law presupposes a common humanity. It only
tries members of our own species. It presupposes, however, a
great deal more than that. In particular it presupposes that the
accused is responsible for his actions. Common humanity does
not determine that issue. It is only of humans that questions
of responsibility can be asked.

mad or bad?
The title of this book, *Mad or Bad?*, suggests that there is a
simple choice: if mad, not bad; if bad, not mad. But it cannot
be as simple as that. For a start, we must distinguish different
senses of madness. If someone were so mad as to count as
legally insane, they would be incapable of forming the intentions
necessary for the imputation of wicked deeds. In such cases,
insanity is a complete defence in law and a total exoneration in
morality. Those who are so disturbed are not to be held
responsible for what they do, nor are they to be personally
condemned. We have the same sort of obligations towards
them as we have to the severely mentally handicapped. So, if

mad, i.e. legally insane, not bad.

Diminished responsibility rests, as we have seen, on mentally abnormal states that do not amount to legal insanity. A person in such a state knows what he is doing and intends to do it. His crimes arise out of his own desires and established traits of character. Yet he may be found to be less than fully accountable for what he does. It may be thought that if a person is not fully accountable for his actions, the only room left for moral judgement concerns the consequences of his actions. This is the idea behind the claim that a person cannot be bad if he is mentally abnormal to the point required for diminished responsibility. The enlightened will treat the psychopath as a natural disaster, comparable to an avalanche or a flood. Regret will be the only rational response. This apparent choice between fully-fledged badness and so-called 'natural evil' may account for the belief that diminished responsibility amounts to some sort of exoneration, and consequently, explains the reluctance to consider a special verdict in the case of such offenders.

The attempt to think of the psychopath as a natural disaster is misguided and unnecessary. We cannot cultivate, and we should not pretend to cultivate, an impersonal attitude to the grossly depraved. The fact that some people are not responsible for their behaviour leaves unchanged our moral attitude not only to their actions and the consequences thereof, but to their characters. dispositions and motivations. If we try to think of a psychopathic assault as a natural event, we leave out what is unbearably painful about the evil involved. The victims of the psychopath are not crushed by some non-human or insensible force. They suffer as objects of human cruelty. It is this that gives our pity for such people a quite different quality from that which we have for the casualties of train crashes. And it explains why it is impossible for the families of victims ever to be reconciled to their fate.

Psychopaths are mad in the popular sense of being seriously mentally abnormal. They are thoroughly bad, in the sense that they intend to do wicked things, they indulge depraved desires and they totally discount the interests of others. Yet they are not accountable for their actions, because no system of human accountancy, moral or legal, can accommodate them. When we attempt to extend to the grossly depraved moral responsibility and guilty verdicts that incorporate moral responsibility, the moral gears grind and eventually seize up. This is not due to our ignorance of the psychology or biochemistry of brutal people. In so far as the law attempts to reflect our basic moral assumptions about responsibility, it has to live with and within the limitations of morality.

notes

Aquinas' theory of damnation can be found in *Summa Theologiae*, 1a 2ae 87, cf. also 1a 2ae 85. The quotations used in this chapter were taken from the English translation made by members of the Dominican Order, under the general editorship of Thomas Gilby O.P. (1964, London, Blackfriars and Eyre & Spottiswoode).

Arendt, H., 1963, *Eichmann in Jerusalem* (London, Faber and Faber).

Babuta, Subniv and Bragard, Jean-Claude, 1988, *Evil* (London, George Weidenfeld and Nicolson).

Diamond M.L., 1960, *Martin Buber, Jewish Existentialist* (N.Y., OUP).

Foucault, M., 1975, *Discipline and Punish* (London, Penguin Books).

Gilbert, M., 1986, *Churchill*, vol. 7 (London, Heinemann)

Levi, P., 1987, *If This Is A Man and The Truce* (London, Sphere Books).

Parkin, D., 1987, (ed.), *The Anthropology of Evil* (Oxford, Blackwell).

Shirer, William L., 1973, *The Rise and Fall of the Third Reich* (London, Pan Books).

Wootton, B., 1959, *Social Science and Social Pathology* (London, George Allen & Unwin).

Yallop, David, 1981, *Deliver Us From Evil* (London, Macdonald Futura Publishers).

index of names